For

Brandon

and all my students who said,

"You need to write a book."

Contents

Chapter 3: Credit 75

Chapter 4: Buying a Car 101

Chapter 5: Renting 131

Introduction

Self-Fulfilling Prophecy

A self-fulfilling prophecy is defined as being positively or negatively influenced by our thinking. I spent thirty-three years in education because I wanted to positively influence young people, and writing this book is the continuation of that goal. Regardless of your age, reading this book will positively influence your thinking and, subsequently, your life. So read on.

The compass is a symbol of guidance and direction, and it serves as a reminder that we can chart our own path in life. Consider this book your life's financial compass. It organizes all of your everyday financial strategies in one place. Your compass will help you answer the what, why, and how when it comes to making sound financial decisions.

The ability to make sound financial decisions is not something we're born with. If we're lucky, we stumble upon valuable lessons accidentally, or even purposely, from our parents. However, the harsh reality is many of them also made mistakes with their finances. Unfortunately, these mistakes can lead to long-term financial consequences. Consequences that we may not be able to reverse or overcome.

What about school? Surely we learned to make sound financial decisions in school, right? Do you believe you were prepared for all of the day-to-day financial decisions when you graduated from high school? What about college?

One of the main reasons I'm writing this book is because most people come out of high school and college without a clear understanding of how to make day-to-day financial decisions. They go through life living in the moment and typically don't truly understand that the decisions they make today may hurt them in the future.

Why is this? In many high schools, we take four years of English, four years of math, and three years of science. These rigorous requirements are important in developing well-rounded young adults. And yet how many years do we spend learning how to make everyday financial decisions?

The answer to this question is different across the United States. Some high schools embed five-week financial literacy concepts as part of a semester-long course that teaches other concepts. Five weeks! Are you kidding me?

Meanwhile, other high schools have students take a financial literacy course that is one semester or half a year. Is this enough time to truly understand all of the important real-life decisions you'll be faced with throughout your lifetime? I've spent thirty-three years working in numerous high schools, and I can unequivocally say ABSOLUTELY NOT!

As a result, most of us are forced to learn as we go. We don't have a solid foundation of financial knowledge, and as such we make mistakes early on in life that stay with us and cause us to have regrets later on. Many of us never gain a good handle on or understanding of our finances. This is really sad to me, and it's why I want to change this for the people who read this book.

From the onset, my goal has been to write a book that is easy to read, easy to understand, and easy to implement. With that goal in mind, I've structured this book in a way that will result in you, the reader, taking action—which will make a great difference in your life.

Introduction: Self-Fulfilling Prophecy

In this book, I've created 40 action statements. Action statements are specific declarations that indicate a course of action. The whole point of the book is for you to TAKE ACTION. These actions will drive your behavior, stretch your earnings, and help you achieve your goals in life. Under each action statement, you will find three simple subcategories.

The first subcategory, the introduction, defines the background knowledge you will need to have a clear understanding of what you're about to read.

The second subcategory, "Why Should I Take Action?" explains the importance of implementing the action statement. The goal of this subcategory is for you to be nodding your head saying, "I get it, and of course I'm going to do this. I'd be foolish not to."

The third and final subcategory is titled "How Do I Take Action?" Here, I describe what you need to do to carry out the action statement. This should answer your questions, guide you, and leave you with a clear understanding of how to actually implement the action statement.

Implementation of all 40 action statements is critical. Why? Because doing so will have a dramatic impact on your life. I believe you'll discover this to be true as you start reading the book.

With 40 action statements in eight chapters, we cover a lot of ground. The chapters include Investments and Retirement, Psychological Spending, Credit, Buying a Car, Renting, Buying a Home, Insurance, and Becoming a Parent: Now What? These eight chapters cover the major financial decisions you will need to make throughout your life.

The book was written for people is their early adulthood ranging from 18 to 34. This is when most young adults make important financial decisions on their own that will have a major impact on their future. That said, anyone of any age can learn valuable lessons from reading this book. Why do I believe this? Because when I enter into conversations with my family, friends, and colleagues about the concepts in this book, most admit they either don't know much about them or aren't very good at implementing them. While I can't protect against losses or guarantee future results, I can unequivocally say that you will learn many important everyday financial concepts from this book.

As you'll quickly understand, it's not *how much* you make but *what you do with the money you make.* As stated earlier, a self-fulfilling prophecy is being positively or negatively influenced by your thinking. Within this book are lessons that will positively influence your thinking, drive your behavior, stretch your earnings, and help you achieve your goals.

Chapter 1

Investments
&
Retirement

Do you want financial freedom in retirement?
The ability to do what you want, when you want,
for as long as you want? You need the financial
resources to make this a reality.

Action 1

I will start investing early for retirement.

Why Should I Take Action?

A successful retirement rarely happens by chance. It happens by design. A wise old man once told me, "If you fail to plan, you plan to fail." You need a plan to have a successful retirement, so let's get started with a short story: the story of Jack and Jill.

Jack and Jill graduated from college majoring in elementary education at the age of 22, and they both share the same birthday. They both get jobs working at local elementary schools. Jack invests $2,000 per year for 12 years and then stops. His total investment is $24,000.

Jill, on the other hand, decides to have some fun with the money she makes from her first real job. She tells herself that after scraping by financially during college, she wants to live a little now that she's earning a paycheck. She wants to buy some clothes, a new car, and go out to eat and to the bars with her friends. Jill tells herself she has plenty of time before she retires, so she delays her retirement investing for six years and then invests $2,000 per year for thirty-seven years. Her total investment is $74,000.

Assume Jack and Jill's return on investment is the same: 10.12%. You may be asking why I chose 10.12%. The S&P 500 comprises the 500 largest publicly traded companies in America. When you hear someone ask, "How is the market doing?" one common benchmark of "the market" is the S&P 500.

According to JP Morgan, the average annual return from 1950 through 2022 is 11.1%.[1] The average annual return for the S&P

500 from 1926 through 2022 was 10.12%.[2] This information is comprised of 96 years of historical data. I'm choosing to use the more conservative number of 10.12% instead of 11.1%. Please don't get bogged down by the rate of return and lose sight of the bigger picture. The overall concept will still be the same regardless of which return on your investment or interest rate you use.

Whose bank account would you rather have when Jack and Jill retire at age 65? Jack will have $1,133,194.22, and Jill will have $857,519.12. Jack invested only $24,000 to Jill's $74,000 and he still has significantly more money than Jill. How can this be?

This is the beauty of compound interest. Compound interest is making money on the money you invest as well as on your returns. Compound interest is the reason it's important to start investing early so you have plenty of time to make money on the money you invested, as well as on your returns. Still not convinced? Let's look again at the importance of investing early for retirement.

In Figure 1-1, we look at investing $100 per month. The numbers are based on the same 10.12% return, which is the historical average of the S&P 500 from 1926 through 2022.

Figure 1-1

Monthly Investment	Investment Starting Age	Total Investment	Amount at Age 65
$100	40	$30,000	$137,543.18
$100	35	$36,000	$235,961.77
$100	30	$42,000	$399,191.66
$100	25	$48,000	$669,912.86
$100	22	$51,600	$911,734.82

The numbers clearly paint the advantage and importance of starting to invest early. In this example, we only invest $100 per month, or $25 per week, and take a close look at the major difference between starting at 22 versus waiting until you're 30 years old.

The difference is more than twice as much and is hard to believe. This should help you understand the beauty of compound interest, which allows you to earn interest on interest over longer periods.

In the next example, we'll look at investing $400 per month, or $100 per week, using the same 10.12% return.

Figure 1-2

Monthly Investment	Investment Starting Age	Total Investment	Amount at Age 65
$400	40	$120,000	$550,172.72
$400	35	$144,000	$943,847.07
$400	30	$168,000	$1,596,766.63
$400	25	$192,000	$2,679,651.42
$400	22	$206,400	$3,646,939.29

Take a close look in Figure 1-2 at the difference between starting at age 25 versus starting at 22. This is an enormous difference from starting only three years earlier. Based on this data, why wouldn't everyone start to invest with their first paycheck right out of college? Surprisingly, in a Bankrate survey, 36% of American workers said they've never had a retirement account such as a 401(k) or IRA. This same survey found that 52% of American workers said they were either behind in their retirement savings, and 16% didn't know where they stand in retirement. This is a combined total of 68% of American workers who are either behind or don't know where they stand. This is not good. Do you know if you are behind? Do you know where you stand? Moving forward, promise yourself to know where you stand in retirement.

Most of my friends and colleagues didn't take advantage of compound interest by investing money for their retirement out of their very first paycheck. Examples of what I heard over and over again included:

"I just graduated from college, and I need to buy new clothes for work. I'll start investing soon."

"I want to have a good time right now. There's plenty of time."

"I want to buy a new car. I'll start investing after I pay it off."

"I want to rent a nice place in the city. I'll start saving for retirement after my next raise."

"I want to travel and then save for a house. Once I get my house, I'll start to invest."

"I just had a baby, and it's expensive. I just don't have the money right now."

Do you know of anyone who struggles in retirement? I know many people who struggled or continued to struggle in their "golden years." Unfortunately, these include friends and family members.

I know many couples who have very little or no money saved for retirement and who live month to month off Social Security.

According to the Social Security Fact Sheet, the average monthly Social Security check in 2022 was $1,669. Who can live on $1,669 per month? The Fact Sheet also shares that among current elderly Social Security beneficiaries, 37% of men and 42% of women receive at least 50% of their income from Social Security.[3]

What happens when the car breaks down or someone gets sick and ends up in the hospital? What if you need a new roof on your home? Life happens, and emergencies happen all too frequently. Social Security is not enough money to live on, and the program was never intended to be the primary source of income in retirement. You also have to ask yourself if Social Security will even be around when you retire. Unless Congress acts and makes changes to Social Security, it is expected to run out of money by 2034.

I also know of people who continue to work into their 70s and even 80s. This isn't because they like to work or want to work but because they have to work. They either need the money now to pay bills or they're worried they won't have enough money when they physically or mentally are unable to work later in life. The longer they work, the greater the likelihood they won't run out of money.

Most people like to feel a sense of control in their life. This is the exact opposite feeling, and it's not a good one. Do you want to retire with financial freedom on your terms, or when you have to because you physically and/or mentally can't work anymore?

The number-one reason people don't retire with dignity is because they make excuses and fail to put money in an account for retirement. They don't implement Action One of investing early for retirement. When I say early, I mean money out of your very first paycheck right out of college. Why? In the example in Figure

1-2, there is close to a million-dollar difference between starting at age 22 versus starting at 25.

You don't need to invest a lot of money. You can start with $25 or $50 per paycheck. Yet most people, including those close to me, make excuses and wait to invest or don't do it at all. Please go back and look at Figure 1-1 and Figure 1-2, and commit to investing right now. Make the conscious decision that will have a MAJOR impact on your life.

If you're like me and need to see the magic of compound interest for yourself, you can go to an online investment calculator and plug in your own numbers to see the beauty of starting to invest early for retirement. The big-picture concept is the same no matter what return on investment you use.

Lastly, to be fair to the people who made excuses, excuses, excuses and didn't start investing early for retirement, ask this question. How many of these people who made and continue to make these excuses actually learned at an early age about compound interest and the importance of starting early? My hunch is very few.

If you're reading this book, you have no more excuses. You can clearly see the importance of starting to invest early to achieve financial freedom. And what is financial freedom? The ability to do what you want, when you want, for as long as you want. Now that is truly a beautiful thing!

How Do I Take Action?

When you graduate from college and get your first real job, you should invest money out of your first paycheck into an employer-sponsored 401(k) (Action 2). If you're currently working and haven't started to invest yet, start immediately by investing in an employer-sponsored 401(k). If your employer doesn't offer a 401(k), then start investing in an IRA (Action 2). Don't continue to make excuses or say, "I wish I would have read this earlier." You can clearly see from the previous examples that the earlier you start, the better off you'll be.

The most important concept in Action Statement 1 is time. Time to let compound interest work its magic. So get started right now. I didn't regret it a long time ago, and you won't regret it either.

Action 2

I will take advantage of retirement saving plans (401(k), Roth 401(k), 403(b), Roth 403(b), IRA, Roth IRA.

Background Knowledge

401(k) – A retirement savings plan offered through your employer in which contributions come directly out of your paycheck and go to investments. Your employer offers a menu of investment options for you to choose from. They may also offer an employer match, which we will go over in Action 3. There are two basic types of 401(k) plans: traditional 401(k) and Roth 401(k).

403(b) – Basically the same as a 401(k), only this is offered to employees of public schools, churches, and other non-profit organizations. These non-profit organizations may not offer an employer match. There are two basic types of 403(b) plans: Traditional 403(b) and Roth 403(b). **Note:** Because a 403(b) operates similarly to a 401(k), I will refer only to 401(k) moving forward.

IRA – Individual Retirement Accounts. There are two basic types: Traditional IRA and Roth IRA. These accounts offer generous tax benefits similar to the 401(k) and are especially good for people who work for companies that don't offer a 401(k).

Stocks – An investment in which you buy a share in the ownership of a corporation. A corporation is a business owned by many people who own stock in the company.

Bonds – A fixed-income investment that essentially represents a loan made by you as an investor to a borrower that may be a corporation or municipality.

Mutual Fund – An investment company that pools the money of thousands of investors and uses the money to buy stocks and bonds. They are led by professional managers and are a good way to diversify. Mutual funds or exchange-traded funds are typically the investment choices for your 401(k).

Exchange-Traded Fund (EFT) – Similar to mutual funds. One major difference is an EFT can be bought and sold like stocks, while mutual funds are bought or sold at the end of the trading day.

Diversification – Not putting all your eggs in one basket; spreading your money around to a variety of investments, which essentially lowers your risk. For example, if you own one stock and the company does poorly, you may lose a significant amount of your money. However, with diversification, you may own stock in 50 companies. If one or even 10 of them do poorly, you can still make money if the others do well.

Why Should I Take Action?

As stated earlier, there are two types of 401(k)s. A traditional 401(k) and a Roth 401(k). We will start with the traditional 401(k) in answering why you should take action. There are two major advantages to a traditional 401(k). These include two terms you may have never heard of: "tax deferred" and "employer match" (Action 3).

Tax deferred allows you to get two significant tax breaks. One is right away and the other is long term. The government allows you to delay paying taxes on the money you contribute to your 401(k). You also get to delay paying taxes on the money that you earn over the years from your investments in your 401(k).

At first glance, this doesn't seem like a big deal, but it's a HUGE DEAL, and one in which you need to take action. For an example of how big a deal tax deferred can mean for you, take a look at Figure 1-3, in which we compare two people. The first person invests their money monthly into a regular investment account. The second person invests their money through their employer-sponsored 401(k) program, which is tax deferred by the government.

You can see in Figure 1-3 how tax deferred savings can add up to an enormous amount of money for you. In this simple example, tax deferred accounted for $308,757.45 more in your account after 40 years. At first glance, the words "tax deferred" may not seem very important, however, in our simple example in Figure 1-3, tax deferred played a major role in achieving financial freedom in retirement.

Please note, tax deferred doesn't mean tax-free. You end up paying these taxes when you start withdrawing the money after age 59 1/2. You may be thinking, *That stinks.* However, another more positive way of thinking about this is that the government is essentially allowing you to use their tax money for 40-plus years. Their tax money is earning you money in compound interest and making your retirement investment amount a whole lot larger because of it. Thank you, Uncle Sam.

If tax deferred were the only major advantage to a 401(k), it would still be well worth investing your money through it. However, there is a second major advantage to a 401(k) called employer match. We'll go into depth on this in Action 3.

Figure 1-3

	Regular Investments (15% Capital Gains Tax)	Investment Through 401(k) (Tax-deferred)
Amount Invested Each Month	200	200
Less Income Taxes	30	0
Left for Investment	$170	$200
Amount Invested After 10 Years	20,400	24,000
Earnings Compounded at 10.12%	14,066.12	16,548.38
Less Tax on Realized Earnings	2,109.92	0
Total Value	$32,356.20	$40,548.387
Amount Invested After 20 Years	40,800	48,000
Earnings Compounded at 10.12%	84,042.41	98,873.42
Less Tax on Realized Earnings	12,606.36	0
Total Value	$112,236.05	$146,873.42
Amount Invested After 30 Years	61,200	72,000
Earnings Compounded at 10.12%	300,625.02	353,676.50
Less Tax on Realized Earnings	45,093.75	0
Total Value	$316,731.27	$425,676.50
Amount Invested After 40 Years	81,600	96,000
Earnings Compounded at 10.12%	901,635.43	1,060,747.57
Less Tax on Realized Earnings	135,245.31	0
Total Value	$847,990.12	$1,156,747.57

The Roth 401(k) is a little different from a traditional 401(k) as it relates to taxes. With a Roth 401(k), you don't get to write off your annual contributions on your income taxes. However, the money you earn in a Roth 401(k) is tax-free. Yes, you read that right: The money you earn is tax-free. In Figure 1-4, we compare investing in a traditional 401(k) versus investing in a Roth 401(k). This is simply showing how much income you have to claim on your annual income taxes.

Figure 1-4

Traditional 401(k)	Roth 401(k)
$100,000 salary	$100,000 salary
$5,000 contribution	$5,000 contribution
$95,000 basis for income taxes	$100,000 basis for income taxes

Based on the numbers in Figure 1-4, you may be wondering why anyone would choose a Roth 401(k). Remember that while you have to pay income taxes up front on the money you contribute to a Roth 401(k), you don't have to pay any taxes on the money that you earn in the Roth 401(k).

How much would you save in taxes? Let's look at an example in which at 22 years old you contribute $6,000 per year in a Roth 401(k) and you continue to do this for 43 years until you retire at age 65. Using the same 10.12% interest, you would end up with $4,773,048.10 at age 65. When you take out your total contributions of $258,000, you're left with earnings of $4,515,048.10.

Let's assume you're married and are in the 24% tax bracket. In this simple example, you would save $1,083,611.54 in taxes. Wow!

Thank you again, Uncle Sam, for creating the Roth 401(k).

After seeing the tax benefits of a 401(k) and a Roth 401(k), you may be upset if your employer doesn't offer either 401(k) options. Don't panic! The government offers similar tax breaks with IRAs. IRAs don't work through your paycheck or even through your employer like the 401(k) does. Instead, you deposit money into the account through your bank.

As stated earlier, there are two types of IRAs. The Traditional IRA works essentially the same way as a 401(k), except it's not done through your employer. However, the tax deferred concept is still the same.

The Roth IRA works essentially the same as the Roth 401(k), except it's also not done through your employer. However, your earnings are tax-free just like the Roth 401(k).

If your employer doesn't offer a 401(k), you can still achieve financial freedom in retirement. Don't use the lack of a 401(k) offering through your employer as an excuse to skip investing early for retirement. You can still invest early through a Traditional IRA or Roth IRA.

In Action 1, we learned about the importance of starting to invest early for retirement. We now build on this concept and take it one step further by understanding the importance of utilizing the traditional 401(k), Roth 401(k), Traditional IRA, or Roth IRA as the vehicle to use for your retirement investments.

How Do I Take Action?

If your employer offers a traditional 401(k) or a Roth 401(k) with an employer match (Action 3), you should contribute to it over the Traditional IRA or Roth IRA.

If your employer offers both 401(k) options, which one should you choose? The two most important variables in making this decision include your age/time horizon before you retire and your tax bracket. In general, Roth 401(k)s are a better choice for young adults for two reasons. First, you have a long time before you retire, which translates into many years of compound interest. Roth makes sense because all of the money you make in this investment is tax-free. Second, you're typically in a lower tax bracket when you're younger.

But even if you're middle-aged, you may still want to take a close look at the Roth option. Why? Because when you withdraw money from your traditional 401(k), it could potentially move you into a higher income tax bracket. The Roth option makes sense for most people.

Don't shut down here. Remember that either option is better than doing nothing. Ask some questions, do a little research, choose one, and start investing in it.

How do you do this? It's quite simple. When you start a new job, the Human Resources (HR) administrator typically will go over the basics of the company's 401(k) offerings. The paperwork to open either 401(k) account typically takes less than 30 minutes.

The good news is that many employers now also offer additional 401(k) assistance through their 401(k) provider and its financial adviser. I've helped some of my nieces and nephews with their 401(k) decision-making and have found these financial advisers to be extremely knowledgeable in helping inexperienced new employees through the process. If your company offers this resource, I strongly recommend taking advantage of it.

A mistake people make is thinking that they need to do more research to fully understand all there is to know about a 401(k), so instead they DO NOTHING. Weeks, months, or even years go by, and they still do nothing. Doing *something* with your 401(k) right away is better than doing nothing. This is a common mistake that you need to avoid at all costs. Just do it! Invest in your 401(k) right away from your very first paycheck!

That said, keep in mind that your company may have a waiting period before you can invest in your 401(k). But as soon as your company allows you to, start to invest.

If you've already started your first job and haven't signed up for a 401(k), go talk to HR and get started right away. We learned the importance of starting right away in Action Statement 1.

When you go to sign up, HR will typically ask you three questions as it relates to your 401(k):

1. Do you want to invest money in a 401(k)? (The only answer should be "Yes!") If your company offers both 401(k) options, you'll also have to tell them which option you want to use.
2. How much do you want to invest per paycheck? (We'll answer this question in Action 3.)
3. Where do you want your money to go?

For question number three, your company will have a list of investment options (typically mutual funds or exchange-traded funds). The list will include company names like Fidelity, T. Rowe Price, and Vanguard to name a few. The list will also include different mutual fund or exchange-traded fund options under each company. For simplicity reasons and because exchange-traded funds are so similar to mutual funds, I will refer only to mutual funds moving forward.

These fund options typically include target date funds, index funds, and actively managed funds. However, the options vary from employer to employer. For example, some employers might not have actively managed funds as an option.

Typically, with the help of the financial adviser, you'll need to choose one of these three options for your 401(k) money. Now let's learn about the three types of mutual funds.

Target Date Fund

A target date fund is a type of mutual fund that gradually shifts assets to a more conservative profile to minimize risk when the target date approaches. The target date typically is your retirement date. Some companies call these life-cycle funds. These funds are for people who don't have any interest in reading about or following markets and investments. You have a mutual fund portfolio manager who is slowly shifting your money to less risk as your retirement date gets closer. You choose one fund and you can be done. You can think of a target date fund as a "do it for me" option. An example of a target date fund is the Fidelity Freedom 2060 fund. You would choose this fund if your year of retirement was 2060. That said, it's not a major deal if you end up retiring earlier or later than this 2060 date.

Index Fund

An index fund is a type of mutual fund that's constructed to match or track the components of a specific type of financial market. An example would be the Standard & Poor's 500 (S&P 500). The manager doesn't actively trade stocks. Rather, they buy whatever stocks or companies are in the index, such as the S&P 500.

This is considered a passive approach, as they continue to buy more shares of the same companies regardless of how these companies are doing. The advantages of index funds include broad market exposure, low operating expenses, and low turnover.

With the target date choice, you choose one fund and let the mutual fund manager take care of asset allocation (Action Statement 6). If you choose to go the index fund route, you need to diversify your portfolio by choosing index funds in different asset classes. Examples of these asset classes include:

- S&P 500 Index – Large Cap Stocks
- Russell 2000 Index – Small Cap Stocks
- MSCI EAFE – International Stocks
- MSCI Emerging Market – Emerging Market Stocks
- Barclays Aggregate Bond Index – Bonds

Whether you're able to choose index funds in five asset classes depends on the investment options provided by your employer. Some employers provide a limited selection and others will have numerous choices, sometimes even multiple choices within these five asset classes.

The advantage of choosing an index fund in each of the five asset classes is diversification. You are not putting all your eggs in one basket. Diversification lowers your risk by spreading your money across the asset classes.

Once you choose your index funds with the help of your provider, you'll need to decide on your percentages. In other words, what percentage of the money coming out of your paycheck goes to each index fund.

Many of the providers now have questionnaires to gauge your risk tolerance (the level of risk you are willing to take with your money) and time horizon, which is also helpful in determining percentages.

In Figure 1-5, we give an example of risk tolerance with aggressive growth having the highest risk and income with capital preservation representing the least amount of risk. These are sample percentages for five index funds based on your risk tolerance.

Figure 1-5

Index Fund	Aggressive Growth	Growth	Growth & Income	Income w/Capital Preservation
S&P 500 Index	62%	53%	41%	22%
Russell 2000 Index	19%	16%	12%	4%
MSCI EAFE International	12%	10%	8%	4%
MSCI Emerging Markets	7%	6%	4%	0%
Barclays Aggregate Bond Index	0%	15%	35%	70%

If your employer doesn't offer any assistance, consider asking for help. For example, I've helped many of my nieces and nephews because they had the presence of mind to ask for help. You could also ask for help from a financial adviser outside of your employer.

To summarize, if you choose the index fund route, choose one fund in each of the five asset classes in Figure 1-5 along with their corresponding percentages. Another way of thinking about percentages is to ask how many dollars of every one hundred dollars will go to each fund. This percentage will be based on the level of risk you want to take. We'll learn more about risk in Action Statement 6.

Chapter 1: Investments & Retirement

This is a lot of information, but don't let yourself become overwhelmed. Stay the course. The 401(k) provider and its financial adviser for the plan should be available to provide some guidance for you.

Actively Managed Fund

Actively managed funds are the third and final option we'll learn about. As opposed to the index fund that mirrors a specific market (S&P 500), portfolio managers are buying and selling stocks and bonds to beat the market (better returns on your investment) of their index.

If you choose to go the actively managed fund route, you can diversify your portfolio by choosing actively managed funds in the same five asset classes as you did for the index funds option. These include:

- S&P 500 Index – Large Cap Stocks
- Russell 2000 Index – Small Cap Stocks
- MSCI EAFE – International Stocks
- MSCI Emerging Market – Emerging Market Stocks
- Barclays Aggregate Bond Index – Bonds or Fixed Income

The difference here is that you would choose actively managed funds and not index funds in these asset classes. You should know if you choose to go with actively managed funds that less than 10% actually beat their benchmark.[4] If your fund or funds are not beating their benchmark, you're better off going the index or target date fund route.

Why would anyone choose this option based on this alarming data? When I started out investing in my early 20s, I chose the actively managed route for my 401(k). At the time, I thoroughly enjoyed reading about the markets and researching mutual funds and their managers. My goal was to beat the market. I spent a lot of time studying and researching this because I enjoyed it. My quest was to beat the market. This is probably not the best option if you don't enjoy this in your spare time.

You'll need to decide with the help of a financial adviser through your 401(k) provider whether you want to invest in a target date fund, index funds, or actively managed funds. Remember, choosing one of these options is better than doing nothing at all. Go back to Figure 1-2 for a reminder of the consequences of doing nothing or delaying your contributions to a 401(k). The reality of starting a 401(k) is that it takes virtually little effort to get started in one.

Keep in mind that you can also change where your money is going at a later date. Some employers allow unlimited changes to your 401(k). Others may limit the number of adjustments per year in the amount taken out of your paycheck, along with where the money's going for investment. Choose where you want the money to go, and do this with your first eligible paycheck. For example, you may change from index funds to actively managed funds or decide later you want to do the target date fund. You can also change from one actively managed fund to another. No worries.

If your employer doesn't have a 401(k), you should choose a Traditional IRA or Roth IRA. How do you do this? You have several options. You can go through a financial adviser or you can do some research yourself and invest directly.

Many characteristics of IRAs will be the same as the explanation for the 401(k). For example, you'll choose a company such as Fidelity, T. Rowe Price, or Vanguard (among many other options). Then you'll choose mutual funds within the company. Similar to a

401(k), you can choose a target date fund, index funds, or actively managed funds. Initially, there will be IRA or Roth IRA paperwork to fill out so you get the tax advantages. You fill out the paperwork and send money to the company and mutual fund(s) you chose.

You then need to decide how much money you want to invest. Because it's not coming out of your paycheck, you have several options. Do you want to send money monthly, semiannually, or annually? You also have the option of having the money automatically withdrawn from your bank account monthly, semiannually, or annually. For example, you can have $100, $200, or $500 taken out of your checking account monthly so you don't forget to feed your retirement account. Setting up automatic withdrawals is an important step in retiring with financial freedom. In 2023, the maximum amount you can invest per year in a Traditional IRA or a Roth IRA is $6,500, and $22,500 for a 401(k). The IRS sets the maximum contribution amount annually, and in some years it remains static.

Those of you who don't have a 401(k) offered to you through work may be upset because you can only contribute $6,500 per year instead of $22,500. Don't lose any sleep over this. If you start to contribute $6,500 per year into an IRA or Roth IRA at the age of 22, you will have $5,170,802.11 at the age of 65. The numbers are based on the same 10.12% return we used before, which is the historical average of the S&P 500 from 1926 through 2022.

The last thing you need to decide is if you want to do a Traditional IRA or Roth IRA. The decision-making process for the Traditional IRA or Roth IRA is exactly the same as the conversation we had for the traditional 401(k) and Roth 401(k), with one exception: The Roth IRA has an income limitation. In 2022, you can't invest in a Roth IRA if you're single and make more than $144,000 or if you're married and make more than $214,000. There are no income limitations for a Roth 401(k).

Remember that choosing to do nothing is the worst thing you can do. Ask a financial adviser or do a little research to decide on a Traditional IRA or a Roth IRA, and start investing. Don't make the mistake of saying, "I don't know which one is better for me, so I'm going to do nothing." As we learned in Action 1, this is the worst thing you can do. TAKE ACTION!!!

Action 3

I will take advantage of my employer
match offered through my 401(k).

Background Knowledge

In the last action statement, we learned about the significant tax benefits of a traditional 401(k) and a Roth 401(k). The other major advantage of a 401(k) is called employer match. This will be true for both the traditional 401(k) and Roth 401(k). For every dollar you invest in your 401(k), your employer will match it dollar for dollar or offer a partial match up to a certain percentage of your salary. Companies do this as a recruiting and retention tool to attract and retain the best candidates. Historically, employer matches have improved significantly over the years.

Fidelity Investments Employer Contribution Trends report for 2020, which was based on 7,506 companies, found the most common employer matching plans were:

- 100 percent match on 3 percent of pay + 50 percent on the next 2 percent of pay (41 percent of plans).
- 100 percent match on 4 percent of pay (15 percent of plans).
- 50 percent match on 6 percent of pay (8 percent of plans).
- 100 percent match on 5 percent of pay (6 percent of plans).
- 100 percent match on 6 percent of pay (7 percent of plans).[5]

It's important to emphasize that the employer match is a use-it-or-lose-it concept. In other words, you only get the employer match money if you put your own money in first. You can't go back years later and try to get the employer match money.

Why Should I Take Action?

Let's start with a real-life story about my niece, who we'll call Anita Job. Anita graduated from Michigan in nursing. She was offered a job with a hospital in downtown Chicago at age 22. The hospital offered her a 5% dollar-for-dollar match on her 401(k). Starting salary for nurses was $60,000, and a 5% employer match on $60,000 is $3,000. Let's take a look at how much just the employer match portion will add up to over her career.

Let's assume the average annual raise for nurses will be 3% over her entire career. Obviously, she may get higher and lower raises throughout her career, but 3% is an average, conservative number. Let's also assume Anita works until age 65 and then retires. She would have a 43-year working career.

The employer match contributions to her 401(k) would be $256,452. However, this number doesn't include 43 years of compound interest. So how much would Anita earn from her employer match portion over 43 years? Let's use the same 10.12% we used in Action Statement 1. Remember, this is the average annual return for the S&P 500 from 1926 through 2022 and represents 96 years of historical data. Anita would have $2,645,401 in JUST the employer match portion of her 401(k). This number doesn't include her own contributions to her 401(k).

Now let's look at Anita's three college roommates who also graduated from Michigan in nursing. They all received job offers from another more prestigious hospital in downtown Chicago. The salary offers were comparable. However, at the time, this hospital didn't offer an employer match. Anita really wanted to get a job at this well-known, more prestigious hospital. However, when I sat down with her and showed her the math with a dollar-for-dollar 5% employer match, her eyes literally popped wide open.

Strictly from a financial point of view, her job with a

comparable salary and a 5% dollar-for-dollar employer match is a much better job offer. Why? I can give you 2,645,401 reasons.

You can see from this simple real-life story that employer match is a big deal. This, along with Action 2 and Action 4, can add up to financial freedom in retirement—the ability to do what you want, when you want, for as long as you want, and have the ultimate resources of time and money to do it.

How Do I Take Action?

When you get your first job out of college and you're meeting with your HR department to go over the paperwork, as stated in Action 2, they'll ask you how much you want to initially contribute to your 401(k).

You should contribute at least enough to get the maximum portion of employer match to your 401(k). This may be dollar-for-dollar or a partial match like 50 cents for every dollar you contribute. If you don't do at least the employer match portion, you'll never see the employer match money ever again. Why would you want to turn away free money? This is like throwing money in the trash. Not a good idea.

For example, if your employer matches dollar for dollar on 5% of your salary and your starting salary is $50,000, you should contribute at least $2,500 (5% of $50,000). Your employer will then match this $2,500 contribution for a total of $5,000 to your 401(k). This $5,000 will earn compound interest and, as you learned earlier with the Anita Job example, can make you a lot of money and eventually offer you financial freedom.

If you don't invest in your 401(k) that year, then neither does your employer. According to Motley Fool, one in five people don't take advantage of the employer match.[6] These people are turning down free money. Your employer will only invest the same percentage, up to 5% in our example, as you do. Doing nothing is essentially giving away thousands of dollars and doesn't help you retire with financial freedom.

If you're older than 22 and haven't yet started taking advantage of your employer match, GET STARTED RIGHT NOW. Don't continue to throw away free money. TAKE ACTION!!!

Action 4

I will increase my 401(k) contributions
every year until I max it out.

Background Knowledge

The maximum annual amount you can contribute to your traditional 401(k) or Roth 401(k) in 2023 is $22,500. Historically, the government re-evaluates its limits every year and will sometimes raise the amount you can contribute.

Why Should I Take Action?

Let me share a story written by one of my nephews, who we'll call Jack Indabox. Jack shares his viewpoint when he graduated from college at age 22 and started his first full-time job:

"After graduating from college where I majored in accounting, I started my first full-time job. On my first day, I received information on my company's 401(k) policy. The Human Resources specialist explained that the company offered a 401(k) savings plan with a company-matching contribution for eligible professionals of $0.50 for every dollar contributed, up to the first 6% of eligible pay per year (e.g., the company contributes 3% of your eligible pay annually if you contribute at least 6%). The HR specialist strongly encouraged contributing at least 6% to fully receive the company match, as this was 'free' money.

"As I commuted home from work that night, the thought of contributing 6% of my salary to a 401(k) plan and having less money deposited into my bank account every two weeks did not excite me. I also found it difficult to think about retirement, as I was only 22 years old and one day into my professional career. However, I kept thinking back to the multiple finance classes I took in college and the importance of a longer time/investment horizon generating much larger profits. I knew prioritizing retirement early in my career would allow me more time with family and friends in retirement as well as being able to travel most of the year.

"Later that night, I found my old college finance book and opened the chapter on retirement plans. The chapter provided an example of two separate individuals investing $19,500 a year into their 401(k) account. The only difference was Individual 1 started investing at 25 years old and Individual 2 started investing at 35 years old. The account balances of Individual 1 and Individual 2 at 70 years old, assuming no distributions and a 6% rate of return, were $4.48 million and $2.32 million.

"The chapter went on to say that the 401(k) contribution limits are expected to continue to rise in the future, allowing individuals to save and invest even more money every year, resulting in more money in retirement. After re-reading the retirement benefits chapter, it was my immediate goal to contribute to the 401(k) limit annually as quickly as possible, as it became clear waiting an additional 3-5 years could potentially cost me millions of dollars.

"The following day at work, I submitted to contribute 15% of my salary to my 401(k) plan. This was the suggested percentage by several financial advisers and ensured I received the full company match ('free' money).

"However, at the time, the 15% contribution did not allow me to reach the 401(k) contribution limit. Since I had just graduated from college and was still unfamiliar with my estimated monthly living expenses, I started tracking every bank deposit (i.e., salary) and expense (i.e., rent, groceries, trips, etc.) to understand my monthly savings. This allowed me to understand how much I could increase my contribution percentage to my 401(k) plan.

"I knew my two largest expenses for the next several years would be rent and purchasing a car. Since I knew a car payment would delay my goal of contributing to the 401(k) limit annually, I only researched cars that I could pay for in cash and eventually purchased a seven-year-old car in cash. As I continued to better understand my monthly savings, I continued to increase my 401(k) contribution percentage until I was able to reach the contribution limit two years after beginning my career.

"In conclusion, researching the impact of delayed 401(k) contributions, understanding my monthly savings (e.g., budgeting), and purchasing a used car in cash to eliminate monthly car payments, allowed me to reach my goal much faster and gave me the peace of mind to know I will be able to retire on my terms one day."

My nephew graduated in accounting and obviously has a clear understanding of the magic of compound interest at an early age. He will have millions of dollars in his 401(k) when he retires. This doesn't include his wife's 401(k) money. They will have financial freedom—the ability to do what they want, when they want, with who they want, for as long as they want. This is OUTSTANDING!

How Do I Take Action?

When you set up your account with your HR administrator or with the financial adviser for your company's 401(k) provider, sign up for automatic escalation, which will annually increase your contribution amount. For example, you can have it set up where you increase the amount by 1%, 2%, 3%, etc. every year. If you get a 5% raise and automatic escalation increases your 401(k) amount by 2%, you will still see a 3% raise in your take-home pay.

If you increase your contributions every year with this automatic escalation, you never see the money in your paycheck. We all adjust our spending habits to how much money we bring home, and setting up additional contributions before you see the money will help ensure that you max out your 401(k), which will lead to your ultimate goal of financial freedom.

If later you decide you want to contribute more or less (hopefully not less) than the automatic escalation, go ahead and make the change. Some plans allow unlimited changes to your 401(k) contributions, and others may limit adjustments to once a quarter or once a year. Some of my nieces and nephews who signed up for this automatic increase realized they could contribute more and filled out the necessary HR paperwork to increase the amount.

For example, in Action 3, we learned about my niece, Anita Job. When Anita started her first nursing job out of college, she started contributing 5% to her 401(k) because she wanted to take advantage of the 5% employer match. She initially didn't want to sign up for more than 5% because this was the first time she was living on her own paying all of the bills, and she wanted to make sure she had enough money to live on.

However, she quickly realized she had enough money to live comfortably so she changed her allocation to 10%. After two years on the job, she received good raises because of a nursing shortage, so she increased her contributions to 15%.

From the beginning, she signed up for a 1% automatic annual increase. When she realized she could contribute more, she made the change.

Moving forward, if she doesn't get as large of a raise, her 401(k) will still automatically increase by 1%. This is important because setting up the automatic increase will prevent her from forgetting to increase her 401(k) contribution in tandem with her raise. Also, because she will never see this extra money in her paycheck, she won't raise her standard of living. This will help her stay the course and eventually max out her 401(k) in a very easy manner.

I share this story with you because I believe it's relatable to most young adults just beginning their careers. I encourage you to do the same as Anita, which is:

- Start investing at least the employer match with your first paycheck.
- Set up an automatic increase on your 401(k) so it coincides with your raises.
- Bring your 401(k) contributions to a conscious level to determine if and hopefully when you can contribute more than the automatic increase.
- Do this every year until you max it out.

You won't regret doing this, as we learned in Action 1, because doing this will allow you to retire with financial freedom. The ability to do what you want, when you want, with who you want for as long as you want. Now that is a beautiful thing.

Action 5

I will have patience and discipline with
the up-and-down cycles of my 401(k).

Background Knowledge

Dollar-Cost Averaging – A well-known investment strategy of investing a fixed dollar amount at regular intervals—$200 every paycheck into your 401(k)—regardless of the share price. The higher the share price, the fewer shares you can buy, and the lower the share price the more shares you can buy and own.

Why Should I Take Action?

No matter what anyone tells you, it's impossible to predict exactly when a stock market decline is coming. Likewise, it is impossible to predict or anticipate when the stock market rebound will happen. Unfortunately, many people wait for the market to drop and then take their money out. Next, they wait until the market improves to get back into the market. No one can time the market. This is extremely challenging because you have to anticipate when to get out of the market as well as when to get back into the market. This requires two decisions to be successfully timed. We don't have a reliable crystal ball, and successfully timing the stock market is nearly impossible even for professional money managers.

I have a good friend who pulled all of his 401(k) money into a cash account with his mutual fund company because he read that the market expected a downturn. However, as it turned out, he missed out on a whole year of good returns because of it. No one can predict exactly when the market will go up or down, regardless of what you read.

From a historical perspective, one of the reasons timing the market is so difficult is the reality that the best trading days tend to cluster close to the worst trading days. Missing some of the best trading days has a surprisingly major impact on your overall return. For example, according to Vanguard, which analyzed data all the way back to 1928, if you missed the 30 best trading days, it would have resulted in half the return. Think about trying to time the 30 best trading days going all the way back to 1928.[7] Impossible!

Let's look at a more recent example of the significance of missing the market's best days using actual numbers. In Figure 1-6, we look at the growth of an initial investment of $10,000 from 1993 to 2022.

Figure 1-6

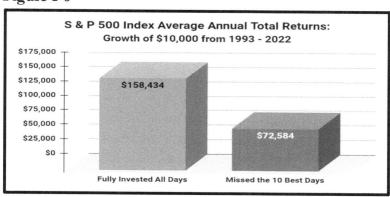

In this simple example, we learn that our $10,000 investment would have grown to $158,434 if we'd stayed in the market the entire time, but only $72,584 if we pulled our money out and missed the 10 best days.[8]

Another very good reason to resist moving your money to cash and to continue feeding your retirement account is dollar-cost averaging. As mentioned previously, dollar-cost averaging involves investing a fixed dollar amount at regular intervals—$200 every paycheck into your 401(k)—regardless of the share price. This strategy takes some of the guesswork out of investing and removes emotions from your decision-making. You're not trying to pick the optimum day to make an investment.

While my friend moved his money out and missed a whole year of stellar returns, he also didn't take advantage of the market slump. One way of staying the course is to consciously view the down market as an opportunity to buy more shares at a lower price. Every paycheck, your fixed dollar amount is purchasing more shares because the price is lower due to the slump in the market. You may be asking, "What if I'm close to retirement and need access to my money soon?" Great question! See Action Statement 6.

You need to remember to have patience and discipline when you see markets decline because you're in it for the long haul. Historically, the market has always come back and made more money. Resist the temptation to get out of the market because you'll miss out on the gains that historically have always come. Stay focused on your long-term financial goals and resist the temptation to obsess over your current account balance. Remember what you learned in Action 1: Time is the best way to capitalize on the magic of compound interest. Time in the market does not mean timing the market.

How Do I Take Action?

This is really quite simple but also extremely hard to do. When the market goes down, you need to resist moving to a cash position. DON'T TOUCH IT! While past performance is no guarantee of future gains, history has shown that it will come back. This is actually fairly remarkable considering the events that have transpired in our history. Will our future crisis be as bad as the Great Depression or World War II? The markets came roaring back after these horrific events.

I choose not to look at how bad it is when the market goes down. This helps me stay the course. During turbulent times, it's natural to want to know how much money you may have lost. However, the more often you check, the more likely you are to make emotional counterproductive decisions. If I look at my 401(k) money and realize I just lost $200,000 in the last two months, I'm tempted to get out of the market. The problem with this strategy is I will surely miss the market gains because how could anyone know the exact start day of the rebound?

You can also remember and tell yourself that a falling market is a buying opportunity because the money coming out of your paycheck is used to purchase shares through your 401(k) at a lower price. This means you can own more shares.

I have a good friend who is an experienced stock trader. I like to talk to him when the market has tanked, as he reminds me to stay the course. I find it comforting coming from someone who does this for a living and is analyzing markets every day.

History has shown us that it's impossible to time the market. While we can't predict the future, history has also shown us that the market will come back after a downturn.

What should you do if you're close to retirement? Should you just leave your money alone? First of all, well done on your critical thinking and analytical skills. But the answer to that question is: Action Statement 6.

Action 6

I will rebalance my portfolio (asset allocation)
to less risk as I get closer to retirement.

Background Knowledge

Asset Allocation – The process of balancing risk and reward in your portfolio by adjusting the percentage of money invested in stocks, bonds, and cash. The adjustments are based on your risk tolerance and time horizon. You can think of risk tolerance as how well you can tolerate the idea of losing money. Time horizon can be defined as how long before you need the money. The longer your time horizon, the more risk you can take, and the shorter your time horizon, the less risk you should take.

Money Market Fund (MMF) – A type of mutual fund that is considered extremely low risk and invests in high-quality, short-term debt instruments. Money Market Funds are also called Stable Value Funds.

Why Should I Take Action?

Asset allocation is important for two main reasons. If you don't take enough risk when you have a long time horizon, your investments may not earn a large enough return to achieve your goals. The opposite is also true. If you take on too much risk when you have a short time horizon, a sudden market decline could prevent you from recouping the money when you actually need it. A good example of a short time horizon would be if you were 55 years old and you wanted to retire at 60 and needed the money to live off for the rest of your life.

When it comes to investing, the higher the risk, the higher the potential reward. Notice the use of the word "potential." In general, stocks are riskier than bonds, and bonds are riskier than cash. However, stocks have a higher potential growth reward than bonds, and bonds have a higher potential growth reward than cash.

Historically, in exchange for the higher risk, stocks have offered the highest return over longer periods. According to JP Morgan, the average annual total return for the S&P 500 stocks from 1950-2022 was 11.1%, and 5.5% for bonds. Figure 1-7 shows the different returns for stocks and bonds over 70 years.

Figure 1-7

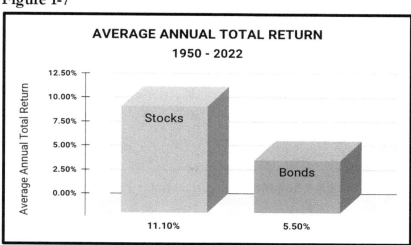

Why do we want to take on more risk when we're younger? Hypothetically, let's look at Bonnie, who invested only in stocks, and Clyde, who invested only in bonds, in their 401(k). They both started right out of college at age 22 investing $250 per month until they retire at 60. In this example, we use the stock and bond historical returns from JP Morgan.

Figure 1-8

Historical Growth of Stocks vs. Bonds	
Bonnie's Investment	**Clyde's Investment**
Stocks (11.1%)	**Bonds (5.50%)**
$1,815,510.63	$387,295.76

You can clearly see the advantage of investing in stocks over the long run. Remember, this is based on more than 70 years' worth of data.

Why do we want to take on less risk as we get closer to retirement? Let's analyze why asset allocation is so important as you move closer to your retirement date. Figure 1-9 looks at the one-, three-, five-, 10-, 15-, and 20-year rolling (compounded) returns of the S&P 500 Index from January 1973 through March 2024.[9] This chart represents over 50 years of data.

Figure 1-9

Chapter 1: Investments & Retirement

If you analyze Figure 1-9 closely, you can see that over short periods, the S&P 500 Index has delivered exceptionally high returns and exceptionally low returns. The best one-year S&P 500 index return was 58%, and the worst one-year return was -43%. Ouch!

However, look at the rolling returns over longer periods. The best 20-year return was 18% per year. The worst 20-year return was 5%. Our 401(k) money is for our retirement and is considered a long-term investment. Based on this historical data over 50 years, we learn the importance of taking on more risk when we have a longer time horizon. Why? In exchange for the higher risk, we can potentially be rewarded with higher returns. While we can't predict the future, history has shown us that this has been the case over a very long period of data.

What about the negative returns in the shorter periods? The data clearly shows that, in the long run, we can make up for money that we lose. The S&P 500 has never lost money in any rolling 15-, 20- or 30-year period.

We also can see that moving our money to less risk as we get closer to retirement is also important. Why would we want to take on the risk of losing money right before we need it?

Time is running out for us to make up the money we may lose in the short term, and we need to take on less risk as we try to minimize the chances of losing money. A good way to think about this is that the young shouldn't invest like the old, and the old shouldn't invest like the young.

Thus, a 20-year-old shouldn't invest like a 55-year-old, and a 55-year-old shouldn't invest like a 20-year-old. Therefore, we must utilize age-based asset allocation to take advantage of risk versus reward and maximize our 401(k) money.

How Do I Take Action?

In Action 2, we discussed target date funds, index funds, and actively managed funds. If you choose a target date fund for your 401(k), then asset allocation is taken care of for you. In other words, you don't need to handle asset allocation because that's the job of the manager of your target date fund. The only thing you need to do is select your target date fund. The manager for the fund will move your money to a lower-risk investment as you get closer to retirement. However, if you choose index funds or actively managed funds for your 401(k), then you or your financial adviser will need to adjust your assets to a lower-risk investment as you get closer to retirement. You will also need to do this if your employer doesn't offer a target date fund in its portfolio.

The easiest way to do this is through your financial adviser. They'll ask you a series of risk-versus-reward type questions to help them determine how to allocate your assets appropriately—this is also called designing your portfolio. They'll adjust this portfolio to less risk as you get closer to retirement. They do this so you take on less risk as you get closer to actually needing the money.

Let's take a look at a sample asset allocation model so you can understand it more fully. There are numerous asset allocation models; this is not a one-size-fits-all situation. This model is a great starting point in understanding how asset allocation works. Don't think of asset allocation as a one-time event. Your allocations will change over time as you get closer to retirement.

In Figures 1-10 and 1-11, we look at a sample asset allocation model from T. Rowe Price strictly based on age. This example doesn't take into account risk tolerance. For example, I was willing to take on more risk than some of my colleagues, so I always had a higher percentage of my money in stocks. These allocations are based on a hypothetical investor who would retire around age 65.

Figure 1-10: Sample asset allocation by age[10]

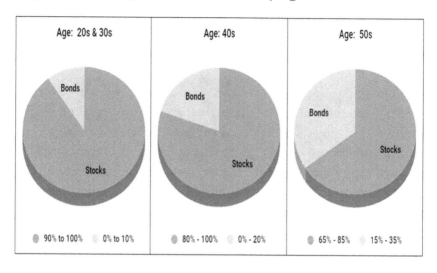

Figure 1-11: Sample asset allocation by age

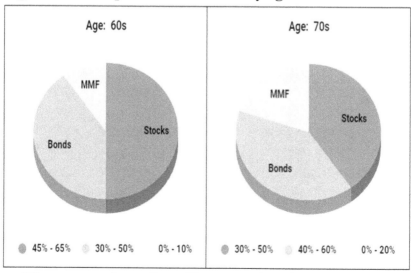

What we can learn from Figures 1-10 and 1-11 is how asset

allocation works. It graphically shows us moving our money from more risk to less risk as we move closer to retirement. This means adjusting our percentage of money from stocks to bonds and eventually moving some money into a money market fund, which is even less risky than bonds.

This is important for two main reasons. First, we want to make sure we take advantage of the higher growth potential of stocks when we're young. This is called capital appreciation. Second, we want to minimize our risk when we get closer to retirement. This is called capital preservation. Doing this can help us retire with financial freedom. The ability to do what we want, when we want, with who we want, for as long as we want. OUTSTANDING!!!

Chapter 2

Psychological **S**pending

Do you want to live a deeply meaningful life? Learn and understand how to create a financial blueprint to help you achieve your vision and your dreams.

Action 7

I will reflect on my lifestyle goals and let those goals be the driving force for my spending habits.

Why Should I Take Action?

Most people I know go through life without consciously prioritizing what's most important to them. They live day by day and make financial decisions in the moment without recognizing that their decisions have an impact on their future. They become emotional or impulsive buyers with a lifestyle that saddles them with expenses.

To better illustrate this, you have to hear the story of Sandy Beach and Rusty Ford. Sandy graduated from college and decided he needed a car for work and pleasure. He always liked the Audi Q5 SUV, so he bought a brand-new Audi Q5 because he could "afford" the monthly payments. He said to himself, "How cool will I look in my Audi Q5?"

Meanwhile, Sandy's buddies planned a vacation to Ireland for 10 days. Sandy really wanted to go along. But he realized he couldn't go because he was spending so much money on very large car payments. He wished he would have bought a used car or even a less expensive new car because Audis are expensive, especially for someone just starting out in the working world.

Sandy's good friend Rusty Ford graduated from college the same year as Sandy. He also needed a car for work. Rusty wanted to travel before having a family. He also believed maxing out his 401(k) at an early age was important to his future. He did some research and learned that a used Honda Accord was the most reliable car and one he wouldn't need to put much money into for repairs. He bought a six-year-old Honda Accord for very little money compared to his buddy Sandy. He also contributed twice as much money to his 401(k) because he didn't have large car payments. He felt fulfilled because he identified traveling and 401(k) contributions as specific goals. The 401(k) contributions are a means to an end because his ultimate goal is to have financial freedom in retirement.

In this simple story, Rusty was able to prioritize what was most important to him and spend his money on those priorities. In contrast, Sandy spent what he had in the moment, which in the end gave him a sense of frustration because he was unable to do the things he truly enjoyed. In reality, he wasn't achieving his goals because he didn't consciously think about what was most important to him. He lived day by day and spent his decreasing discretionary income on his next want or desire. Thus, Sandy became an emotional or impulse buyer.

How Do I Take Action?

The reality for most working adults is that there is not enough money to do everything we want to do in life. Take some time to reflect on what's most important to you. What are your goals in life? Ask yourself the following thought-provoking questions as you go through the visionary exercise.

Questions: What is Most Important in Life?
- Do I like to drive fancy cars?
- Do I like to travel?
- Do I like to go out to dinner?
- Do I like to go to concerts or sporting events?
- Do I want a large, expensive wedding?

- Do I want to have a family?
- How many children would I like to have?
- What traditions do I want to carry on with my family?
- What are some new traditions I want to implement with my family?
- Do I want to initially rent in a really nice high-rise in the big city?
- What type of house do I want?
- Do I want a second home on a lake?
- Do I want a boat, jet skis, snowmobiles, or other "toys"?
- What hobbies do I want to be able to do?

Questions: What is Most Important in Retirement?
- What do I want my retirement to look like?
- Do I want to ratchet up my traveling?
- Do I want to travel around the world?
- Do I want to go RVing?
- Do I want a second home somewhere warm for the winter?
- Do I want a second home in the mountains?
- Do I want to live on or near the ocean?
- Do I want to live on a lake and have a fishing boat, pontoon boat, or sailboat?
- Do I want to pay to take my children and/or grandchildren on vacations?
- Do I want to pay for my grandchildren's college educations?
- Do I want a simple retirement living close to my grandchildren?
- Is there anything else is important to me not mentioned?

If you have a significant other in your life, you should discuss these questions together to determine what's most important to you. It does you no good if you're on one page with your financial goals and your significant other is on another. I have a good friend who's not on the same page with his wife on goals and spending. He eloquently described it as "very stressful." He feels like he's trying to plug holes in a ship where the captain (his wife) continues to ram into icebergs. This is not a healthy situation.

Now take a look at your goals document and turn them into more formal written life goals. These life goals give you a sense of day-to-day direction. For example, one of my life goals included, "I want to maximize my 401(k) because I want to have financial freedom in retirement." Because I wrote this down, I made it a priority and it actually happened. It didn't happen by happenstance. It happened because I made a conscious decision to make it happen.

Asking these questions should help you prioritize your goals so you actually make them happen. Have a written blueprint or vision and then follow this vision with your spending habits.

I also think it's important to internalize these goals and keep them front and center. One way to accomplish this is to create a goals document that you can look at more frequently to remind you of the most important areas in which to spend your money. I like to post this goal document on a small cork board I have above my desk. This keeps me focused and keeps me from becoming an emotional or impulse buyer.

This vision should guide you and give you a sense of direction when you need to make daily financial decisions. For example, if cars are not important to you, then buy used cars (Action 12). This will allow you to have more money for goals that are more important to you. If cars are really important to you, then buying new or leasing your cars may be the direction you want to go. We just need to realize and clearly understand that buying new or leasing cars frequently means we have less money for other things in life.

As mentioned earlier, there is an old saying: "If you fail to plan, you plan to fail." I've found this to be true throughout my life. Think about who and what really matters to you. Family is most important in my life, and the financial ability to do the things we love to do together became part of my personal blueprint and vision as I asked myself the previous thought-provoking questions.

To that end, the three things related to finances that were most important to me included living in a beautiful home, traveling, and most importantly retiring with financial freedom.

Take some time to create your financial blueprint and vision so you aren't frustrated like Sandy. This is time well spent and should make day-to-day financial decisions much easier for you and your family. Going through this exercise will bring your dreams and goals to a conscious level. This in turn will help make your dreams a reality and ultimately a deeper, more meaningful life.

It's worth noting that this is not a one-time exercise. You should continue to assess your goals and change your spending habits as you go through the different stages of life. For example, your goals will change when you get married, or when you have your first child. Come back to these thought-provoking questions periodically to help clarify what's most important to you and your family.

Action 8

I will consider opportunity cost when making spending
decisions and live below my means.

Why Should I Take Action?

Opportunity cost is the price you pay or what you give up
when you make a financial decision. In Action 7, we learned
the story of Sandy Beach buying a fancy Audi Q5. His opportunity
cost, or what he gave up because he bought the fancy car, resulted
in a lower amount of money going to his 401(k) and the inability
to go with his friends on a trip to Ireland.

While we didn't talk about it, his future opportunity costs also
included the lack of resources to save for a down payment on a
home and other upcoming expenditures. The reality is that Sandy
has less discretionary income because he's living day by day and
making impulsive or emotional spending decisions.

Let's take a look at the smaller decisions made by Ann Teak.
Ann and her husband took Action 7 to heart. They went through
the thought-provoking questions and decided together that retiring
with financial freedom and having a beautiful home are their two
most important lifestyle goals.

Ann enjoys iced caramel macchiatos from Starbucks, but she
also recognizes that $6 every day equates to more than $2,000 a
year. She decides that the opportunity cost is not worth it to her
because she doesn't like macchiatos as much as retiring with financial freedom and having a beautiful home. She forgoes the everyday macchiato purchase. This conscious decision saves her $2,000
a year every year for other more important goals in life.

This simple decision to forgo a macchiato purchase every day makes her feel good because she took the time to assess what was most important to her in the long term. Unlike Sandy Beach, Ann is not an emotional or impulse buyer. As a result, she doesn't feel the frustration of not being able to accomplish her goals because she actually brought those goals to a conscious level and then considered opportunity cost with her buying decisions. This helps her live below her means.

Let's look at another opportunity cost example from my brother-in-law, who we'll call Bert Toast. When he was 23 years old and fresh out of college, Bert thought it would be amazing to have independence from his parents. He never went through Action 7 and never thought through all of his life goals or what was most important to him.

Bert bought a townhome down the block from his parents. This was a knee-jerk impulse-buying decision. He lived in the home for one year. The problem was he didn't have enough extra money to do anything with his friends. Hence, the opportunity cost of wanting independence and buying this home was the inability to go out with his buddies, which is important at the young age of 23. He had to give up living in the townhome because most of his money was going toward paying the mortgage.

After a year of missing out, Bert decided he had made a mistake and moved back home to live with his parents. He was able to rent the home to someone else for a couple of years before eventually selling it.

In hindsight, the whole experience was a downer for him as he missed out on a year of experiences with his friends and then was forced to move back with his parents. He initially couldn't afford the house even though the bank gave him the money to buy it. Getting in over his head was a learning lesson that stayed with him.

Later in life, he married, and when he and his wife went to look at houses, the bank was willing to let them borrow enough money for a more expensive home. They wound up buying a less expensive home because of the lesson he'd learned when he was 23.

From that point forward, he understood how his decisions had ramifications for his future. Bert knew when they had children, his wife would probably stay home and they would be living on one income.

Moving forward, we can all learn from these three stories. Consider opportunity costs when making buying decisions, and live below your means. Consciously ask, "What am I giving up by making this purchase? Does this purchase fit into the overarching goals that I laid out in Action 7?"

Considering opportunity costs will help you make sound rational buying decisions that match your goals. This will give you a sense of satisfaction because you're spending your hard-earned money on the things that are most important to you and ultimately not spending more than you make in a month.

How Do I Take Action?

First, take action on Action 7 and analyze your goals so you know what's most important to you in your life. Second, bring opportunity cost to the forefront of your thought process. Think about your goals and decide if spending money on your current wants and desires is worth the opportunity cost. This should be easier because you actually have your goals in writing and can refer to them often. You may even want to post your goals somewhere for you to look at every day.

When I was growing up, my dad would frequently repeat the old saying, "Don't try to keep up with the Joneses." He wasn't referring to one of my cousins whose last name was Jones. He was referring to impulse buying and letting our desires and wants overtake our actual needs. Another way of saying this is to live below our means, which is spending less than we make each month.

I took this saying to heart and didn't fall into this vicious trap. However, I watched many in my warm circle fall into this trap. One such example is a couple who bought a really expensive home despite not making as much money as some of my other friends. They eventually lost the home to foreclosure, which created a hole so large they never really financially recovered from it. Take the wisdom from my dad and "don't try to keep up with the Joneses."

To that end, take 10 seconds and make a conscious effort or a habit of mentally thinking though opportunity costs. I believe you'll feel more fulfilled having a clear vision of what is most important to you and your significant other. In reality, your good friends and family will respect you because you're a kind, compassionate person and not because you can "keep up with the Joneses" with the type of car you drive or the house you live in.

Don't believe me? Take a minute and think about who you enjoy being around most. Is it someone who drives a nice car or lives in a beautiful home? Or is it someone who is kind and compassionate and takes an interest in you and your life—someone who is a good listener and asks thought-provoking questions about you and your family?

Chapter 3

Credit

Do you want to save literally tens of thousands of dollars in interest payments to a bank? Learn and understand the importance and the ins and outs of credit.

Action 9

I will establish and maintain good credit.

Background Knowledge

Credit – Receiving goods and services now with a promise to pay in the future.

Credit Report – A summary of your personal credit history. Equifax, Experian, and TransUnion are the three credit bureaus that collect credit data on you and provide lenders your credit report and credit score.

Credit Score – A numerical expression between 300 and 850 (the higher the better) that tells lenders how likely you are to pay back the money borrowed. Your score is primarily based on your credit report. In Figure 3-1, we look at what the different credit score numbers mean.

Figure 3-1[11]

Credit Score	Rating
Below 580	Poor
580 - 669	Fair
670 - 739	Good
740 - 799	Very Good
800 and above	Exceptional

Credit Card Minimum Payment – The lowest amount you can pay every month while keeping your credit card account in good standing. The amount is typically 1% to 3% of the card balance. Interest starts accruing immediately when you don't pay your credit card in full every month.

Grace Period – The period between the end of your billing cycle on a credit card and the date your payment is due. This is typically 20 to 30 days on most credit cards.

Annual Fee – The money you have to pay every year for certain credit cards. Most credit cards don't charge an annual fee. However, annual fees are more typical with cards that offer perks, such as airline miles or cash-back opportunities.

Why Should I Take Action?

Are you a trust fund baby? In other words, do you have so much money in your 20s and 30s that you don't need to borrow any money or take out a loan for the rest of your life? Can you pay cash for your home and cars?

Almost all of us answer "no" to these questions. As a result, we all have to borrow money throughout our lives. At the very least, we need to borrow money to buy a car or a house, as well as utilize the convenience of credit cards for everyday purchases like groceries and going out to dinner.

Having a good credit score drives many things in our lives. I know lots of people who are surprised and even shocked when they learn just how much is driven by our credit scores.

The obvious question is: What happens when you don't establish and maintain good credit?

To start with, you will pay higher interest rates when you

purchase a home. A friend of mine has been a mortgage broker for more than 35 years.

He gave me the data in Figure 3-2, which represents $250,000 borrowed on a 30-year fixed loan (Action 20).

Figure 3-2

Credit Score	Interest Rate	Monthly Payment	Total Interest Paid
650	7.625	$1,769.48	$387,014.37
690	5.625	$1,439.14	$268,090.76
740	5.375	$1,399,13	$253,974.11

In Figure 3-2, you learn that 40 or 50 points on our credit score plays a significant role in the interest rate you'd be able to get when purchasing a home.

Would you rather pay $387,014.37 or $253,974.11 in interest for your home? This $133,040.26 difference is all based on our credit score. Can you think of other ways you'd rather spend $133,040.26?

Having a low credit score also means you'll pay higher interest rates when you purchase a car.

Another friend of mine is a general manager for an automobile dealership, and he's been in the car business for more than 30 years.

The following data is from one of the banks his dealership works with and is based on a used car loan for a car that is 2017 or newer with a loan term of 48 months (four years).

Figure 3-3

Credit Score Range	Interest Rate
775+	4.00%
774 - 725	4.79%
724 - 675	5.34%
674 - 635	6.49%
634 - 595	11.49%
Less than 595	12.69%

Let's take Figure 3-3 and go one step further with an actual example of borrowing $20,000 for a car on a four-year loan.

Figure 3-4

Credit Score Range	Interest Rate	Monthly Payment	Total Interest
775+	4.00%	$451.58	$1,675.89
774 - 725	4.79%	$458.69	$2,016.92
724 - 675	5.34%	$463.67	$2,256.28
674 - 635	6.49%	$474.21	$2,761.93
634 - 595	11.49%	$521.68	$5,040.76
<595	12.69%	$533.48	$5,606.94

Similar to the home loan, why would you want to have a $533.48 monthly car payment when you can have a $451.58

monthly car payment simply by maintaining a good credit score? The difference in total interest paid for this car example is $3,931.05. I come back to the same question I asked on your home loan. Can you think of other ways to spend $3,931.05 instead of giving a bank more money?

The mortgage broker and the automobile dealership general manager, independently from one another, also stated that people with low credit scores have fewer loan options available to them when purchasing their homes or cars. This is important because limiting your choices will also cost you flexibility and ultimately money.

Yet another factor that's influenced by a low credit score is the higher rates you'll pay for auto and home insurance. My brother is an insurance agent, and he was able to lower a customer's home-owners insurance policy by $387 for the year simply by using the husband's credit score instead of the wife's. The wife had good credit, but the husband had exceptional credit. He was able to save another couple $546 on their annual auto policy premium and $276 on their homeowners policy because the customer's credit score increased by 125 points. This is an annual savings of $822. Can you think of other ways you could spend $822?

The other reality is that insurance companies may decline to offer you coverage if your credit score is too low. They may not want to take the risk.

Other consequences of having a low credit score include:

- Not having access to premium reward credit cards.
- Utility companies can charge you a deposit when you have a poor credit score.
- Some landlords may choose not to rent an apartment or house to you, or they may make you pay a higher deposit if they choose to take the chance to rent to you at all.

My brother and I owned several rental homes. We made the decision not to take the chance on renting to people with less-than-stellar credit. Why would we when we had plenty of applicants to choose from?

Low credit scores may also hurt your chances in a job hunt in certain careers where the company runs your credit report. For example, one of my nephews is a certified public accountant. His firm ran a credit report on him before they hired him.

Now let's summarize the impact on someone who chooses not to establish and maintain good credit:

- Pay higher interest rates on homes.
- Pay higher interest rates on cars.
- Pay higher auto and home insurance rates.
- No access to premium reward credit cards.
- Forced to make a deposit with utility companies.
- Landlords may not rent to them.
- May lose a job offer.

Wow! That's a whole lot of negative repercussions for having a bad or low credit score. Why, then, would anyone not establish and maintain a good credit score? The American Bankers Association keeps quarterly data on credit cards. Analyzing their data shows that between 53% and 60% of people with credit cards carry a balance in the most recent quarters, which ultimately hurts their credit scores. Don't fall into this trap.

Many don't realize the negative ramifications of having a lower credit score. However, after reading this section, you've learned the importance of establishing and maintaining a good credit score. Now you need to TAKE ACTION and actually make this happen.

How Do I Take Action?

First, we need to look at how credit scores are calculated.

Figure 3-5[12]

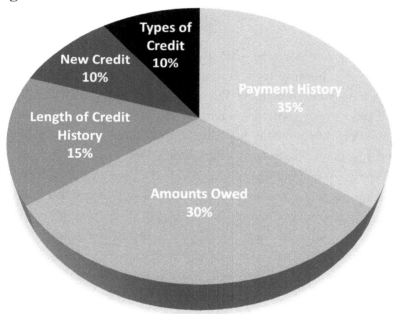

- 35% Payment History – Do you pay your bills on time?
- 30% Amounts Owed – This is calculated as a percentage based on available credit vs. how much credit is used. Creditors do not want to see you max out your available credit or reach your credit limit. Try never to exceed 20-30% of your credit limit.
- 15% Length of Credit History – This looks at the duration of time you've had your accounts open. The longer the better. This is why it is so hard for younger adults to have a high credit score.

- 10% New Credit – Opening several new credit accounts in quick succession will hurt your credit score.
- 10% Types of Credit – Creditors like to see you're able to handle different types of credit accounts. For example, credit cards, auto loans, school loans, and mortgages are all different types of credit accounts.

Starting out as a young adult is challenging as it relates to your credit score because how do you build a credit history when you don't have a credit history? The answer is to start small and build. You can start out with a small credit card ($500 to $1000), use the card every month, and pay the entire balance off every single month. This will help build your credit score.

Apply for a small loan (auto) and make your monthly payment on time every month. You can do this even if you don't need to borrow the money. On the other side of the spectrum, if you don't qualify for a loan because you're young and just starting out with your first job, you can have a co-signer help you get the loan. Keep in mind that your co-signer will be on the hook if you don't make the payments.

You can have monthly utility bills and cell phone bills in your name and pay the bills in full every month. All of these examples build your credit score.

The single most important factor in establishing and maintaining a good credit score is paying your bills on time. This includes paying your entire credit card balance in full every month and not paying just the minimum or leaving a monthly balance. Even though your credit card monthly statement indicates that you only have to make the minimum payment, don't do that because it will hurt your credit score. Credit cards have a minimum payment amount because the companies want you to pay the minimum balance so they can start to charge you interest on the balance that's left. The bad news is the interest rate is typically extremely high.

To illustrate how important paying your bills on time every month is, I want to share a true story from one of my close friends, who we'll call Howie Duen. Howie was purchasing a new Tesla; the company was offering a 0.9% interest rate promotion. However, despite having a good credit score, they told him they couldn't offer him the 0.9% interest rate because his credit report showed a late payment on his Target card. Because he was late once, they said the best they could offer him at the time was 3.9%.

Howie was dumbfounded. He thought he always paid his bills on time. When he investigated the situation, he found the Target card charge was for $7 and that there had been a mix-up with the payment. Still, the $7 charge was technically paid back late. Think about this. Because he was late one time in his life with a $7 charge, his interest rate on a brand-new vehicle went from 0.9% to 3.9%. This is thousands of dollars in extra interest. Hopefully, you can learn from this real-life example and understand the importance of paying your bills on time.

To pay your bills on time, you'll need to live within your means. Don't overextend yourself to the point where you can't pay your entire credit card balance off each month, and don't be late with a loan payment or utility bill. It's important to delay gratification. You can also use a two-credit-card cut-off system described in the next action statement.

Remember the ramifications. In the long run, the consequences of higher interest rates on auto loans and mortgages—paying more in auto and home insurance rates, and all the other negatives—are not worth it. It really is quite simple. Spend what you can afford. To do this, you'll need to resist impulse buying and concentrate on your overarching goals in life.

To completely maximize your chances of having the highest credit score possible, go back to the pie chart in Figure 3-5 and reread the descriptions underneath it. This is the system of how credit scores are calculated. Internalize this system and make it a goal of yours to work on raising your credit score. As we learned throughout this action statement, it's well worth your time and effort to bring this to a conscious level and TAKE ACTION on raising your credit score.

Action **10**

I will pay my credit cards in full every month.

Why Should I Take Action?

We just learned about the importance of establishing and maintaining a good credit score. Understanding how much of an impact your credit score can have on your life, why would I include the action item of "I will pay my credit cards in full every month"? This is a thought-provoking question and two thumbs up to those readers who figured it out.

The reason I created a separate action item on this concept is because the statistics show most adults don't pay their credit cards off every month. I want you to learn and understand the true importance this will have in your life. To that end, I want to show you the impact of carrying a balance on your credit card will have on your finances above and beyond hurting your credit score.

According to Lending Tree, the average annual percentage rate (APR) for new credit card offers is 22.91% and the average APR for all current credit card accounts is 16.27%. These may fluctuate one way or the other. However, what we need to understand is that credit cards charge very high interest rates when compared to interest rates for our homes and cars.

Why do I say that? For many years you could buy a home for 3% or 4% interest. In 2022 (Action 12) that creeped up to around 6%. In good times, you can also purchase a brand-new automobile with 0% financing. Compare this to the 22.91% average on new credit card offers. This is outrageous and one of the ways credit card companies make large amounts of money off of you. But they don't have to, and they won't if you don't let them.

Credit card companies entice you to start making high-interest payments by offering a "minimum payment" figure on your monthly credit card bill. They know that many people are short on cash and may struggle to pay their credit card balance in full every month. Remember, the minimum payment is typically a very low amount, or 1% to 3% of the credit card balance. In Figure 3-6, we look at making the minimum payment of 2.5% with a 17% interest rate on our credit card.

Figure 3-6

Balance	Time to Pay Off	Interest Charged	Total Amount Paid
$1,000	12 years	$979	$1,979
$2,500	19 years	$2,941	$5,441
$5,000	24 years	$6,210	$11,210

Really analyze the chart and internalize how much interest you have to pay on high-interest credit cards. Does this really help us stretch our earnings and achieve our goals?

Still not convinced? Let's look at another example in writing and not in chart form. Let's look at impulse buying gone amok. What would it look like if you decided you had to have that big-screen television for the Super Bowl and charged $2,000 on your credit card? You know you don't have the money to pay it back, but you really want the TV because you want to impress your friends.

What would it look like if you made the required minimum monthly payment with a 19.8% interest rate and a $40 annual fee?

It will take you 31 years and 2 months to pay the credit card off, and you will pay $8,202 in interest.

That's a significant amount of money for a TV, and you'll be a whole lot older when you finally pay it off. Was it really worth it? Was a $2,000 big-screen television worth an additional $8,202 in interest? Do you think your friends really like you better because you have a big-screen TV? Go back and internalize the consequences of carrying a balance on your credit card. TAKE ACTION and spend what you can afford.

How Do I Take Action?

This is really quite simple and yet so hard for so many people. On one hand, all you need to do is limit what you charge to what you can afford to pay off each and every month. This is easy to do if you can eliminate your wants and desires from the equation. You need to find a way to get rid of your impulse buying and come back to your overarching life goals. If you took the time in Chapter Two to really think through your goals and even put them in writing, you know these goals are what you ultimately decided are most important to you.

Don't try to keep up with the Joneses. Honestly, your real friends and family won't like you better because you have a big-screen TV, a new sweater, or whatever you're charging on your credit card and can't actually pay off in full every month. Your real friends and family will like you better because you're a caring, thoughtful, and compassionate friend who takes an interest in their lives.

Believe me, I completely understand money can be tight, especially when you're just starting out with your first full-time job right out of college. You may feel like you need so many things in life. When money is tight, you can also utilize a two-credit-card cut-off system. I utilized this system right after college and when I was first married. It allowed me more time to pay my credit cards in full every month. (I practice what I preach; I've always paid my credit cards in full every month. This was true even when money was tight because I'd just started working and didn't make very much money.)

How the system works is you stagger two credit card cut-off dates. The cut-off date represents the day of the month your credit card company will total the amount you charged for that month and send you a bill. For example, your MasterCard cut-off date can be on the 15th of the month and your Visa can be on the 1st of every month. Credit card companies will allow you to determine the cut-off date. You can just call them to make changes to your existing cut-off dates.

Credit cards have a grace period, which is the period between the end of your billing cycle and the date the payment is due. When your credit card is in the grace period, you won't be charged interest on your purchases as long as you pay your bill in full within the grace period. Grace periods typically are 20 to 30 days after the cut-off date.

How do we use the staggered cut-off date system? In this example, you make charges (that you can afford to pay in full) on your MasterCard (cut-off date is on the 15th) on the 16th through the first of the next month. You make charges on your Visa (cut-off date is on the 1st) from the second of the month through the 14th. What this gives you is more time to pay the bill in full every month. In the meantime, you'll get one or two paychecks and have more time and money to pay your bills within your 20- to 30-day grace period.

The staggered cut-off date system worked really well for my wife and me when we didn't make very much money. It gave us time to get paid, which ultimately allowed us to pay our credit card bills in full every month. The end result was a higher credit score and all the major advantages that come with that.

To summarize, resist impulse buying, charge what you can afford, use a staggered cut-off date system when money is tight, and pay your credit card bills in full every month so you can maintain a higher credit score. Doing this will allow you to gain access to all of the advantages of higher credit scores. Now all you need to do is consciously make this happen. TAKE ACTION!

Action 11

I will research and choose the best
reward credit card for my circumstances.

Why Should I Take Action?

In Action Statement 9, we learned the major advantages of establishing and maintaining a good credit score. This includes paying off your credit card in full every single month.

I know many people who apply for credit cards based on an application that was sent to them through the mail. This is especially true with college-aged students.

Credit cards target college students because they want them to use their company's credit card for the rest of their lives. They'll send you multiple credit card applications in the mail, hoping you'll fill them out. It's worth their time and money to do so because they get so many students applying.

They may offer you something free if you fill it out. They may also hire some of your fellow college students to set up a booth in the quad or in the student center and give you something for free if you fill out an application.

You need to resist the temptation to do so. Remember what you learned in Action 9: Filling multiple credit card offers actually hurts your credit score.

Let me illustrate by sharing a story about myself as an example for choosing a rewards credit card. I didn't simply fill out an application for a credit card I received in the mail. I also didn't fill out applications from my peers who had booths set up in our student center. Instead, I researched what credit card matched my goals in life.

One of my goals was to have my family experience all the must-see sights and must-do attractions in all 50 states. We love to travel. To that end, I have a travel rewards credit card that at the time of my research offered the most travel miles for my everyday purchases.

We charge everything in my family, and I mean everything. We then pay the balance off in full every month. Doing this typically allows us to go on at least one trip per year where my travel reward miles pay for the airfare somewhere in the United States. Essentially, my airfare is free for the convenience of using the credit card for my everyday purchases. If we go on a driving trip, my travel reward miles will pay for the hotels.

Doing this has saved us thousands of dollars in travel costs and has also allowed us to go on trips more frequently. This also helps my family save money, stretch our earnings, and travel. Thank you, rewards credit card, for helping my family make this goal a reality.

How Do I Take Action?

Let me start by saying that many of these reward credit cards will require you to have a good credit score. This is another reason to establish and maintain a good credit score (Action 9).

Look for websites that compare reward credit cards. Beware of websites that exist solely to promote their own credit cards.

Next, decide what rewards you're most interested in, as all credit cards offer different types. Some offer discounts on hotels, rental cars, airline miles, and cash back on purchases to name a few.

Remember, as we learned in Action 9, opening new credit cards hurts your credit score, so don't apply for a whole bunch of reward credit cards. I have two credit cards that I've had for most of my adult life. I use my reward credit card for all of my everyday purchases and only use my second credit card if there's something wrong with the chip on my reward credit card. This is a very rare occurrence, but having the second card comes in handy in such situations.

Most people use credit cards for convenience purposes, but as we've learned, many people also use them because they don't have the money to actually pay for goods and services. If you're using a credit card for convenience purposes, you should also reap the rewards of using a credit card by taking advantage of the rewards offered. There is no interest charged when you pay in full every month, and using the card can actually help you save money, stretch your earnings, and achieve your goals faster.

It's worth noting that most reward credit cards charge an annual fee. My reward card charges me $90 for the use of their credit card. I did a cost-benefit analysis and determined the $90 annual fee is worth the benefit of having my family airfare paid on at least one vacation every year.

Action 12

I will look at what the Federal Reserve is doing with interest rates before buying a home or car.

Background Knowledge

The Federal Reserve (Fed) will raise the federal funds target rate during inflationary times to increase the cost of credit (borrowing) throughout the economy. Higher interest rates make loans more expensive for individuals and organizations, which discourages borrowing and in turn cools down the economy. This will eventually bring down inflation.

The Federal Reserve will also do the opposite and lower the federal funds target rate during recessionary times (not enough spending and higher unemployment) to decrease the cost of credit (borrowing) throughout the economy.

Lower interest rates make loans less expensive, which encourages borrowing. In turn, people and businesses spend more money. This increased spending prompts businesses to hire more people to handle the increased demand, which helps lower the unemployment rate and bring our economy out of a recession.

You may have not been aware of this before reading this book, but the raising and lowering of the federal funds target rate takes place regularly.

To illustrate the drastic changes made to the federal funds rate, Figure 3-7 gives you a historical perspective from 1980 to 2020.

Take a close look at how much the rate has changed over time. Also, look at how high and low the rates have been over time, as this is significant in understanding the importance of this action statement.

Figure 3-7[13]

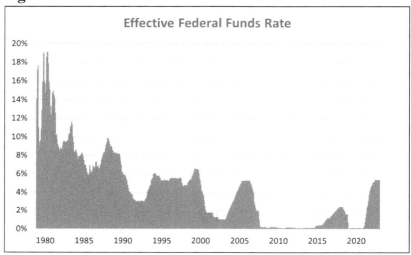

Why Should I Take Action?

Typically, the two largest purchases in our lives are our home and automobile. We should always be aware of what's going on around us—or, put another way, what's in the news. This should include what the Federal Reserve is doing with interest rates. Why is this so important?

To answer this question, let's look at Figure 3-8, in which we borrow $250,000 on a 30-year fixed-rate mortgage to buy our first home. We'll learn more about a 30-year fixed-rate mortgage in Action Statement 23. Figure 3-8 illustrates how our monthly mortgage payment and the total amount of interest paid to a bank for our home changes with the interest rate change.

I set the lowest interest rate at 2.65% because historically, that has been the lowest 30-year fixed interest rate (2021). I set the highest interest rate at 18.45% because it has historically been the highest 30-year fixed interest rate (1981).[14]

To break it down even further, in 2022, interest rates started out at 3.45% in January and rose to 6.9% in October. When you analyze Figure 3-8, you can see your monthly payment would be $530.85 more, and over the life of the loan, your total interest would be $191,107.65 more in October of 2022 compared to January of the same year.

Figure 3-8

Interest Rate	Monthly Payment	Total Interest Paid
2.65	$1,007.41	$112,667.41
3.00	$1,054.01	$129,443.63
3.45	$1,115.65	$151,632.47
4.00	$1,193.54	$179,673.77
5.00	$1,342.05	$233,139.46
6.90	$1,646.50	$342,740.12
18.45	$3,859.64	$1,139,469.01

Ouch!! That's a whole lot of extra money to live in the exact same home. Does the potential of paying $530.85 more per month and $191,107.65 more in extra interest make it worth looking at what the Federal Reserve is doing with interest rates? ARE YOU KIDDING ME? YES!!! Doing this will save you an enormous amount of money, stretch your earnings, and help you achieve your goals faster.

How Do I Take Action?

Over my lifetime of buying homes and automobiles, my wife and I generally know when we're interested in buying a home as well as when we need a different car.

However, our timeline typically has some flexibility built into it. In other words, we don't have to move to a different home this month, and we don't have to purchase a different car this month.

I listen to the news when they talk about the Fed, and what the Fed is thinking or has done with interest rates. I don't typically get my news online, but some of my friends do, and I've shown them what to look for with the Fed news as well.

You can do a search for "Fed news" to get a pulse on interest rates. You'll probably be surprised at how much will show up when you do a Google search. I know many of my friends have been surprised, as they never really paid much attention to the Fed in the past.

The Fed usually doesn't make knee-jerk decisions. Rather, they warn us far in advance what they're thinking about doing in the future with interest rates.

Just by paying attention either on TV or searching online, you can learn whether interest rates are trending upward or downward, and you can gain an understanding as to why they're heading in that direction.

Having this knowledge can help you decide if you should move quickly or wait a few months to buy that house or car. This may seem trivial.

However, looking at Figure 3-9, we learn that it's not. Look at how much a 30-year fixed-rate interest rate changed from January 3, 2022, to October 24, 2022.

Figure 3-9

| 3.22% | 4.72% | 5.81% | 7.08% |
| January 3, 2022 | April 4, 2022 | June 20, 2022 | October 24, 2022 |

In Figure 3-10, we analyze what impact a change in interest rates had from January to October 2022 on a 30-year fixed-rate mortgage where we borrow $250,000.

Figure 3-10

Interest Rate	Monthly Payment	Total Interest
3.22%	$1,083.90	$140,205.36
4.72%	$1,299.60	$217,856.54
5.81%	$1,468.48	$278,651.00
7.08%	$1,676.71	$353,615.52

In this simple real-life example, your monthly payment increased by $592.81, and the total amount of interest paid to a bank over the life of the loan increased by $213,410.16. OH, MY!!! This seems hard to believe, and yet this truly represents the difference in buying a home in October instead of January. The same would be true for auto interest rates.

Why would you want higher monthly payments and ultimately pay more interest over the life of the loan when you don't have to? All you have to do is keep your eyes and ears open to the Fed, and you'll have the knowledge to make better-informed financial decisions. This knowledge will save you money, stretch your earnings, and help you achieve your goals faster.

Chapter 4

Buying a **C**ar

Is it financially better to lease, buy a new car, or buy a used car? Learn and understand how to get the best deal and the ins and outs of purchasing and maintaining your car.

Action 13

I will research reliability before I purchase a car.

Why Should I Take Action?

Not all cars are created equal. Reliability ratings are based on how well vehicles have held up in the past and the odds that you can expect problems or repairs in the future. I've driven some make and model vehicles for 200,000 miles without having to spend money on repairs other than routine maintenance. Routine maintenance includes oil changes, tires, brakes, batteries, and fluid changes at the appropriate mileage intervals.

Unfortunately, I've also owned a vehicle that required repairs beyond routine maintenance. I made the mistake of purchasing a car because I liked the look of it and shied away from the reliability ratings. I regretted this decision and will never do it again. I also have some friends who made the same mistake of falling in love with the look of a car while ignoring the reliability ratings. They also had the inconvenience as well as the unfortunate expense of wasting money on having the car repaired.

Let's begin with some examples. A friend of mine spent $3,000 to have his car's transmission rebuilt. The repair shop told him they see a lot of this particular model.

I had a car that had electrical problems, and I spent $1,500 having it repaired. If I had researched the reliability of the car's make and model before buying, I would have found that it had a history of electrical problems.

While these were one-time expenses, a more typical experience is a car that "nickel and dimes" you over its lifespan. This can add up to a significant amount of money. This is also a major headache and very inconvenient when you have to drop the car off and be without it for one or more days.

Why would you want to spend money on repairs when other models have proven to be much more reliable? This is a waste of money. Doing a little research to find a reliable make and model is well worth the time spent and will save you money, stretch your earnings, and help you achieve your goals faster.

How Do I Take Action?

This is really quite simple. Start by doing a Google search on the most reliable car brands. You'll find all kinds of data from a variety of sources on the brands that consistently produce highly reliable cars. Examples of brands include Chevy, Ford, Honda, Nissan, and Toyota to name a few. Please note that these are examples of brands and not necessarily the brands I recommend.

I also recommend narrowing your search even more by Googling the most reliable car models. Examples of car models would be Accord (Honda), Blazer (Chevy), Camry (Toyota), Explorer (Ford), and Rogue (Nissan). Once again, these are examples of models and not necessarily the ones I recommend.

You can also go to some specific independent industry-recognized consumer research companies like Consumer Reports, J.D. Power, and Repair Pal. These companies will give you reliability ratings based on cost, frequency, and severity of actual unscheduled repairs. You can compare and contrast different brands and models to see which have the fewest problems.

I learned the hard way that doing a little research on vehicle reliability can go a long way in saving frustration and money on unscheduled repairs. Ultimately, it comes down to this: Why spend money when you truly don't have to?

Action 14

I will do my research and be prepared when I walk into a car dealership so that I will pay the least amount of money possible.

Background Knowledge

The automobile industry was hit really hard with supply chain issues during the COVID-19 pandemic. This caused automakers to cut production of new cars. As a result, demand outpaced supply, which caused prices to rise faster than inflation. The action statements in this chapter are based on normal economic conditions.

MSRP – Manufacturer's suggested retail price. This is the price you'll see on the sticker in the window for a new car. This doesn't mean you have to pay this price. It's a suggested price from the manufacturer. I've never paid MSRP for a car. You can pay less for almost all cars during normal times.

Invoice Price – What the dealer paid for a new car.

Trade-in – How much your used car is worth when trading it in.

Private Party – The price of a used car when you are selling the car to a person other than a car dealer.

Dealer Retail – The price of a used car when the dealer is selling the car. Dealer retail is what you should pay for the used car and not more than it's worth.

Destination Charge – The fee the manufacturer charges the dealer to ship the car to the dealer. This is included in the price of a new car, as the dealer passes it on to you.

Why Should I Take Action?

The car business is one of the few in which two people can walk into the exact same car dealership on the exact same day and pay dramatically different amounts of money for the exact same make and model. These two people can literally drive their car down the road having paid thousands of dollars difference.

So many people walk into car dealerships without first doing any research. They essentially walk in blind without knowing how much they should pay for the car. This makes no sense to me, as typically a car will be the second-most expensive purchase we make in our lifetime other than our homes.

I also know people who tell me they "got a good deal" on their car purchase. When I ask them how they know they got a good deal, they typically look at me and don't have a good answer. This tells me they have no idea if they got a good deal or not. It's more their gut talking to them, which is not the same as getting a good deal.

The best way to get a good deal and not overpay for a car is to do your research first. You need to know how much the dealer paid for the car if it's a new car, and how much the car is worth if it's a used car. You also need to know how much your current car is worth if you're trading it in or selling it yourself. Having this knowledge will ultimately let you know whether you really "got a good deal" or not.

The average person will own approximately six cars in their lifetime. If you're married, that means the two of you may own around 12 cars in your lifetime. If you can save $2,000 per car, that means you could save as much as $24,000. That's money you could invest to make more money or spend in other areas of your life that are important to you and your family.

If you knew you could save $24,000 by doing a little research each time you bought a car, would you be interested? Most people I know say "yes" to this question. Why? Because it helps you achieve your goals faster.

How Do I Take Action?

We'll separate this action statement into two: buying a new car and buying a used car.

Buying a New Car

If you want to pay the least amount of money for a new car, you first need to know how much the dealer paid for the car. This is called the dealer invoice price.

You can go to websites like Edmunds.com and kbb.com (Kelley Blue Book) to do your research. In fact, I recommend using both so you can compare and contrast the valuable information given.

These websites are also good sources to learn about the car's reliability, reviews, safety, exterior and interior options, as well as looking at pictures and videos of different car options. Go to these websites after you've researched the vehicle's reliability (Action 13).

Lastly, you can use these websites to learn if there are any incentives on certain models. Incentives may include cash back or money for new college graduates, special financing rates like 0.9% interest, or $5,000 cash back from the manufacturer. I use these websites to narrow down my choices and ultimately use the information to choose which make and model car I want to buy.

These websites change frequently, so I won't go into how to navigate them. You'll need to explore a bit to get the information you need, but it's worth it to save thousands of dollars each time you purchase a car.

To find out what the dealer paid for the car (dealer invoice), you'll have to enter all of the options you want on the car to get an accurate price. You should also add the destination charge (shipping) to this price.

Once you know what the dealer paid for the car, you can walk into the dealership knowing what you want to pay. We will go in-depth on how to take this dealer invoice number, negotiate, and get a good deal in Action 15.

Buying a Used Car

You can go to a website like Autotrader.com to find a used car close to your home. I still find it worthwhile to go to Edmunds.com or kbb.com to do research first on what make and model car I want to buy based on reliability and reviews, as well as my own preferences. I use these websites to figure out what a specific car on Autotrader.com is worth. You'll find many of the cars listed for sale are from dealers who may have them listed for much more than you should pay for them. Find out how much the car you want should sell for before going into the dealership to negotiate and ultimately buy the car.

When I'm purchasing a used car, I also think it is worthwhile to go to a website like carfax.com and get a CARFAX vehicle history report. This report will tell you if the car you're looking at has ever been in an accident as well as maintenance done on the car. I would shy away from a car that's been in an accident. Having been in several accidents myself (none were my fault, no really, true story!), the car never drives the same way after it's been in an accident.

I also use Edmunds.com and kbb.com to figure out how much my own car is worth. It does you no good to do all kinds of research on buying a car if you don't know how much you should get for trading in your old car. You need to figure out both to save the most money on the overall car purchase.

Please remember that you need to be honest when figuring out how much your current car is worth. The websites will ask for vehicle condition, and it's not realistic to say your car is outstanding when in reality it's in average or even rough shape. The websites will give you a description of what outstanding means along with the other qualifiers. If you're honest, you'll get an accurate value of what your car is worth. I used a really old car from one of my nephews in Figure 4-1 to demonstrate the difference in value based on the condition of the car.

Figure 4-1

Condition	Trade-In	Private Party	Dealer Retail
Outstanding	$2,221	$3,323	$5,195
Clean	$1,343	$2,037	$3,213
Average	$1,927	$2,899	$4,520
Rough	$1,151	$1,738	$2,720

Figure 4-1 shows you the different values and how you'll be able to get more money when you sell your car yourself (private party column) rather than trading it in. The numbers were taken directly from one of the two car websites, and as you can see, they'll tell you how much your car is worth if you're trading it in or what it's worth if you sell it directly to a consumer.

Selling directly to a private party is obviously a lot more work, and you need to decide if it's financially worth it. Fortunately, it's become easier with websites like Autotrader, where you can list your car for sale. The dealer retail column tells you how much you should pay if you purchase this car from the dealer.

You should also know that your sales tax is less when you trade a car in as they subtract the trade-in value from the purchase price of the car. You can figure out if it's worth your time and hassle to try to sell it yourself or not. Honestly, when I was younger, I sold the cars myself and as I grew older and had more discretionary income, I made the decision to trade my cars in. This is your decision, but know that you will get more money by selling it yourself.

Doing research before you walk into a car dealership will give you the information necessary to negotiate (Action 15) a "good deal" on your next car purchase. You will see that this action statement becomes more important and is directly tied to the next action statement.

Action 15

I will utilize effective negotiation
strategies when buying a car.

Background Knowledge

General Manager – Oversees all aspects of the daily operation of
an automobile dealership. One of those aspects is the price you
end up paying for the car. Salespeople typically don't have the au-
thority to sell you the car at a certain price. They need to go to the
general manager, who is empowered by the owner of the dealership to sell the car to you for a specific price. In most dealerships,
the salesperson will get up from where you're sitting and leave you
to check with the general manager. They usually go back and forth
multiple times before a price is agreed upon by you and the general
manager.

Finance Office – Once you agree on the price of the car, you will
go into the finance office to take care of all of the paperwork, insurance, finances, and add-ons.

Why Should I Take Action?

I've bought numerous cars throughout my life. I've also helped
my sisters, nieces, and nephews buy cars. As a result, I have a
considerable amount of experience dealing with car dealerships. I
point this out because my experience has taught me that most (not
all) car dealers, or at least the ones I've dealt with, will take advantage of you financially if you let them.

I've found success in the car-buying negotiation process. This
success has allowed me to pay the least amount of money possible

so I can use the money saved to do more rewarding things in life other than making a car dealer more money. I've also saved my relatives a lot of money so they can do the same.

Just because the automotive dealer is asking $25,000 for a used car doesn't mean it's worth $25,000. What if I told you the car you're looking at, which is priced at $25,000, is only worth $20,000? Would you be willing to learn how to negotiate so you could save $5,000? YES!!

How Do I Take Action?

The goal of car salespeople is to make the most money they can on a car. Your goal is to pay the least amount of money on your car purchase so you can use the money on other goals in life.

You need to start by asking which department makes the most amount of money for a car dealership.

Analyze Figure 4-2 and think through which departments typically make the most money for an automobile dealership.

Figure 4-2

Automobile Dealership Departments	
Department	**Description**
Finance Office	Handles all of the paperwork, insurance, finances, add-ons and extended warranties
New Car Sales	Selling customers new cars
Parts Department	Replacement parts for your car
Service Department	Handles maintenance and repairs
Used Car Sales	Selling customers used cars

What do you think? Which department makes the most money for a dealership? I've asked this question to hundreds of people, and most people say new car sales.

The reality is that most car dealers don't make the bulk of their profits from new car sales. In fact, that ranks near the bottom of overall profits for most dealers.

Most make a large percentage of their money from car loans, selling add-ons and extended warranties in the finance office, service work, and your trade-in vehicle.

Why did I share this with you? Because your mindset entering negotiations is the first concept you need to address. Many people go into a car dealership with the mindset that the car dealer has to make money when they purchase a new car from them. This is absolutely not true and the wrong mindset.

Car dealers don't need to make money on you from your new car purchase. A more accurate representation is that they want to sell you the car so they can make money off of you in the finance office. (Which they won't—not after you read Action 16). They also want to sell you the car because they want to make money when you bring it back for service. If you don't buy the car from them, then typically they can't make money from servicing your car.

I've always walked into a car dealership with the mindset that they don't need to make one penny from me on the sale of the car. This has served me well, as I've always bought my cars at dealer invoice price for new cars and fair market value for used cars. This is worth repeating. The dealer doesn't need to make one penny from you in the sale of the car. This is the mindset you need to have walking into the dealership. I cannot stress how important this is in the negotiation process.

I didn't buy a car during the COVID-19 pandemic, nor would

I as car dealers had supply chain issues. These negotiation strategies don't work during supply chain issues. I told my immediate family that we were not in the market for a car and wouldn't be until things went back to normal. Buying a car in bad times like COVID-19 just means you're paying more for the same car. If you wait, normal times will return and you'll save money.

Now that we have the proper mindset walking into the car dealer, let's discuss negotiation strategies that have worked very well for me and should work for you.

1. As discussed in Action 13, you need to first do your research. Research includes finding which make and model you plan to purchase. Remember this should include a look at reliability because the last thing you want to do is buy a car that you have to put money into because of maintenance issues. This will hurt your finances and your ability to achieve your goals.

Research pricing. This includes what the dealer paid for the new car, how much your used car is worth on a trade-in (you can sell it yourself and make more money), and the dealer retail price if you're buying a used car (you'll save a lot of depreciation on a car if you buy a used car).

You should also research any dealer incentives available like special financing or cash-back offers on certain models. If there are no special financing offers, then you want to research auto interest rates at various banks before you walk into a dealership. It's no good to negotiate a good price on a car and then use dealer financing if they're charging you 3% interest when a local bank is charging only 2%. This could add up to $1,000 or more on what's called the "back end" of the car deal. Do your research on reliability, pricing, incentives, and interest rates before walking into the dealership.

2. Once you've done your research, you may still not be sure which new car you want to buy. You may have narrowed it down to two models. Go in and do a test drive. It won't cost you anything. I strongly recommend that you tell the salesperson you plan to buy a new car and are just test-driving cars. They still may try to pressure you into buying a car from them without test-driving other cars. Just keep repeating to them, "I'm only test-driving today. I'm only test-driving today."

If you're buying a used car, you'll need to test drive several used cars. Again, tell the dealer you're just test-driving cars today. If you find a used car you like, you still need to go home to figure out what the car is worth so you can get a good deal. You'll go home and research to find the dealer retail price on the used car and then go back to the dealership to negotiate the price.

3. When is the best time of the year to buy a new car? For most cars, the new models typically start arriving in the fall. So October is a great time to buy a new car. Next year's models are arriving, and dealers want to get rid of the new models from the previous year. I've bought cars at this time of year and have succeeded in buying them below the dealer invoice price. This is always fun.

4. I like to walk the lot on a Sunday when car dealers are closed and make sure the dealer has the make, model, and color I want. This makes for hassle-free looking around the lot. You also want to do this because car dealers are more likely to sell the car to you at the dealer invoice price if they have the car on their lot. It will cost them more money to get the car from another dealer, and they'll want to pass this cost on to you. Make sure the car is on the lot before negotiating a price.

The Financial Compass

5. I like to walk into the dealer showing my checkbook as well as the price information from the research I've done. The checkbook tells the salesperson I'm ready to buy today. It can be from them or another dealer down the street. I've also found that negotiations go a little easier when they can visibly see that you know what they paid for the car. Don't hide this information. Show them that you know the dealer invoice price, or what the dealer paid for the car. This also goes for the paperwork on how much your trade-in is worth.

6. Hold your ground! Always stick to the dealer invoice price. They will try to get you up from this price, but don't budge or even move up $50. Once you move even a little bit, they'll try to get you to move some more. It's a process, and the process is designed to wear you down and come up on your price. Don't do it. Just hold your ground.

This is uncomfortable for some people. One time, I was negotiating for my sister, who had the money for the car. The dealer and I were $400 apart on the price.

The salesperson said, "Let's split the difference."

I said, "Absolutely not."

He walked away to go talk to the general manager again. My sister hit me in the arm and said, "STOP, I hate this, give him the $200!"

I said, "Don't worry, he'll eventually sell us the car at our price."

The salesperson came back with the general manager, who tried to get us to go up by $200. When I wouldn't back down, he stood up and shook my hand, saying, "You have a deal." Remember, this took a while to get them to agree to our price. They have to try to get us to agree to a higher price because it means more profit for them. Afterward, I told my sister she owed me a steak dinner.

116

7. Know the names of other dealers who carry cars from the same manufacturer. One time, I was going through negotiations, and after a really long time, we were at an impasse. Neither of us were budging. So I told him I was going to go to the competition to buy my car, a dealer located in the neighboring town. The salesperson stood up and said, "Wait a minute, just wait a minute." He went and brought back the general manager, who tried one last time to get me to come up in price. When he realized I wasn't budging, he stood up, offered me a handshake, and said, "I'm not going to have you tell all your neighbors you went to the next town over to buy your car." He was right. I would have been asked why I didn't buy the car in my hometown. This is not good for business. He knew it and I knew it. Remember, they want to sell you the car.

8. Always give the salesperson your name and number. One time, I left a car dealer because I wouldn't budge on the dealer invoice price and they weren't coming down. I went home, and guess what happened? The very next day, I received a phone call from the salesperson asking me if I'd bought a car yet. I told him not yet. He said they'd sell me the car at my price if I came back in. I did, and I got my price. It took a little extra work, but it was worth it.

9. Always talk about the price of the car you're buying first, trade-in second, and financing third. Many salespeople will mix all three numbers together to confuse you. They're better at negotiations than you are, as they do this every day all day long.

I like to separate the negotiations into three separate processes. When they ask me if I have a trade-in, I say, "I'm not sure yet." This allows us to talk only about the price of the car I want to buy. It's much easier to focus on just one number at a time. After we agree on the price (which is the dealer invoice price), I say, "I would like to trade in my car." Now we are only talking about one number again: how much my used car is worth. You should do your research ahead of time and have the information printed out so the salesperson knows you know how much your car is worth. Stick to this number. They'll try to say your car isn't in good condition and don't think it's worth what the true value of the trade-in is. To be fair, you must be honest about the condition of the car. However, if you're being honest about its condition, don't budge on this number. HOLD YOUR GROUND! Remember, they truly want to sell you a car today. They'll make you work for it, though, and this will take some time. It's all part of the process, and the process is meant to wear you out and have you pay more money.

10. If you've been there awhile and it doesn't appear as though you're going to get a deal done, stand up to walk out. Don't make the mistake of doing this too early. You have to let them try to get more money out of you first for this strategy to work.

I've done this many times, and all but once, the salesperson said something like, "Wait a minute, just sit down, just sit down and let me try one more time." They'll come back with the general manager, who will try to get me to come up in price.

When I hold my ground, the general manager sells the car to me at my dealer invoice price. They think they'll make some money off me in the finance office, which they won't (Action 16), and eventually on service.

11. If you don't enjoy the negotiation process, bring someone with you who does. If you still don't like it, try online buying, where dealers send you their prices. I have never bought online because I've always done well going in and negotiating.

These negotiation strategies have always worked for me. This is not an exhaustive list but numerous strategies that have helped me save my hard-earned money for other goals in life and not waste it by making a car dealership more money from me. They'll make their money from me when I take my car in to be serviced.

Action 16

I will not waste my money
in the dealer finance office.

Why Should I Take Action?

Once you agree on a price for a car with the salesperson and general manager, you will then go into the finance office. These people work with contracts and numbers all day long, and I've found them to be very sharp.

In my experience, most of these people will use questionable methods and even lies to get you to spend more money. They'll try to sell you extended warranties, fabric protection, paint protection, rustproofing, and VIN etching to name a few. They will tell you, "Everyone or most people go with it." This is not true, and even if some people are gullible enough to buy it, it doesn't matter because you should know better after reading this action statement.

Do you really think your brand-new car will rust out if you don't pay $300 to have the paint sealed? Don't you believe manufacturers already have a high-quality finish on the car? What about extended warranties? In my experience, when you read the fine print on these documents, they're a waste of money.

All of the dealers I've worked with when buying a car have tried to get me to buy an extended warranty. I once had a finance officer really go after me hard to buy an extended warranty. He was putting unbelievable pressure on me to purchase the extended warranty for $1,500. It was truly uncomfortable. I then told him, "I must be buying the wrong brand-new car if you're telling me it's going to break down. I guess I need to go buy a Toyota." He stopped trying to get me to sign for an extended warranty and moved on to the rest of the paperwork.

These add-ons are a complete waste of money and can cost you hundreds or even thousands of dollars. For example, I had a close friend who paid $1,495 for paint 3M sealant, $495 for interior Scotchgard and leather conditioner, and $495 for sound and undercoating. This is a grand total of $2,485 above what he paid for the car. This was several years ago, and he has since sold the car. Did he really get $2,485 worth of products, or was this a complete waste of money? I have never bought anything being sold in the finance office other than the actual car, and I have never regretted it. DON'T buy them.

I've also found that some of these finance officers will "make a mistake" on the paperwork. The sales contract is filled with numbers, including the price of the car, the price of your trade-in, the down payment, the interest rate, and the terms of the loan. Always double-check these numbers. I've found mistakes on these sales contracts. When I've questioned it, the finance officer says something like, "Oh, I'm sorry, it was an honest mistake." In my opinion, this was no honest mistake. It was purposeful to make more money from our transaction.

Don't waste your money on add-ons in the finance office, and always check the numbers to make sure there are no "mistakes" on the paperwork.

How Do I Take Action?

When you finish with the salesperson, they'll have you wait to see the finance officer. Numerous salespeople have told me things like "It's easy from here" or "You're in good hands now." Nothing could be further from the truth, as these are skilled high-pressure salespeople. They want you to let your guard down.

The best way to handle your finance office experience is to be guarded at all times. Don't buy any additional items that aren't needed and aren't worth it. Double-check and verify all the numbers. The whole process is designed to wear you out. You now know better. Remember, no matter what they say, you don't need to buy anything regardless of the amount of pressure they put on you. JUST SAY NO AND CHECK THE NUMBERS! Doing this will save you thousands of dollars, which can be spent on other goals in your life.

Action 17

I will recognize the opportunity cost and value in purchasing used cars over new cars and leasing.

Background Knowledge

Automobile Leasing – Essentially, you are renting the car from a car dealership for a certain dollar amount and length of time (most typically three years).

Why Should I Take Action?

We'll start with leasing a car and then move to buying a brand-new car. When you lease a car, you always have a car payment. You never build any equity in the car you're driving because you never actually own the car. You're renting it, and when your lease is up, you turn the car in and start all over with lease payments. Essentially, you never get to sell the car and use this money to buy a different car.

While there are some advantages to leasing a car, like always driving a new car, strictly from a financial point of view, you're better off buying a used car. This will allow you to use the saved money to do something else.

However, if driving new cars is one of your life goals (Action 7), then leasing may be for you. I just want you to recognize that leasing will be more expensive and eat up more of your resources than buying a used car. The opportunity cost of leasing a car is less money for you to use elsewhere.

Let's now look at buying a new car. New cars lose their value the minute you drive them off the lot. How much and how quickly they depreciate depends on many factors including make, model, condition, mileage, and ownership history. Most cars will lose 20% of their value within the first year and another 15% per year for the next three years. That's a whole lot of depreciation in the first four years of a car's life cycle.

Cars are better built now than they ever have been. Early on in my driving experience, we drove our cars for 100,000 miles before having to put money into them. It's not uncommon today to get closer to 200,000 miles before having to spend money on a car. This is especially true if you've researched reliable car makes and models.

All cars need routine maintenance like oil changes, batteries, brakes, and fluid changes at certain mileage points. When I refer to spending money on cars, I mean beyond routine maintenance.

Let me use a real-life example of the opportunity cost and value of buying a used car over buying a new one. In Action 4, we learned about my nephew, Jack Indabox, who maxed out his 401(k) contributions at age 24. He talked about purchasing a used car to max out his 401(k). Let's now look at the specifics of his car purchase. He purchased a 2007 Honda Accord in October of 2014. When he researched used cars, he discovered that the Honda Accord was one of the most reliable cars at the time. This was important because my nephew didn't want to be pouring money into a used car that was breaking down.

The car he purchased had 69,716 miles on it, and in 2022 it had 138,774. He spent no money on the car other than routine maintenance like gas, oil changes, tires, and brakes. He paid $11,312 for the car. A brand-new Honda Accord at the time would have been $23,545.

He saved $12,233 because he bought a reliable used car over a new car. He also was able to pay cash so he had no car payments. This allowed him to use the money he would have spent on car payments to help him with his goal of maxing out his 401(k).

You can see there's a snowball effect here. By purchasing a reliable used car, my nephew:

- Saved $12,233 on the purchase price of his car.
- Has had no car payments for the last ten years and counting, as he's still driving the car.
- Used the money he saved on the purchase price and no car payments to maximize his 401(k) contributions (Action 4).

His decision to buy a reliable used car right out of college at age 22 is a gift that will keep on giving. He had no car payments, and yet he has a reliable car that gets him from place to place. His decision to buy a used car and use the money he would have spent on a new car to max out his 401(k) will pay huge dividends when he retires.

As we learned earlier about the magic of compound interest, this literally could be a six-figure decision. This real-life example illustrates the opportunity cost and value of purchasing used cars over new cars and leasing. Why? New cars depreciate significantly in the first three years, and you always have a car payment when you lease.

How Do I Take Action?

As you learned in Action 14, you need to do your research using websites like Edmunds.com and kbb.com (Kelley Blue Book). Research how much you will save if you buy a three- or four-year-old car with low miles vs. buying a brand-new car in whatever make and model you're considering.

You saw that my nephew saved $12,233 just by buying a used car rather than a new one. You also saw in this real-life story that he's had no car payments for the last ten years. This savings, or opportunity cost, allowed him to do other things with his money including maxing out his 401(k) contributions (Action 4). This was a goal of his (Action 7) that allowed him to save money, stretch his earnings, and achieve his financial goals a whole lot quicker than he would have had he purchased a new car with car payments. Now you have to ask yourself: What would YOU do with the money saved from buying a used car?

Action 18

I will find an honest, reliable, and
affordable automotive repair shop.

Why Should I Take Action?

In Action 13, we learned about the importance of doing exten-
sive research on reliability when purchasing a car. I cannot stress
this enough. The best thing you can do with this action statement
to save money, stretch your earnings, and achieve your goals is to
buy a reliable make and model car.

Now that you own a reliable car, you will eventually need to
have routine maintenance done and possibly some unscheduled
repairs. To that end, why would you want to spend time researching repair shops? Let's answer that question with a few stories.

I once had my vehicle in the dealership for warranty work, and
besides doing the warranty work, most dealers will also typically
perform an inspection of your vehicle to let you know what else is
wrong with the car. This is pretty typical no matter where you go
and a way for the dealership to make more money off you on repairs.

The dealer told me my timing cover was leaking oil and needed
to be resealed, which would cost $1,434.87. I told them not to do
the work. I then took my car to someone I trusted to give me an
honest assessment of my car. He inspected the car and told me the
timing cover wasn't leaking oil, but the turbo feed line gasket was
leaking, which was right above the timing cover. Hence, the oil on
the timing cover was coming from the turbo feed above the timing
cover.

The cost to replace this gasket was $71.13. My repair went from

127

$1,443.87 to $71.13 because I went to my honest, reliable, and affordable mechanic.

Another time, I had a dealer tell me that my car needed new brakes, which is part of routine maintenance. He wanted to charge me $1,100 for brake pads and rotors. I took the car to my trusted repair shop and was told I could drive the car for another 10,000 miles before the brake pads needed to be replaced. I did drive the car another 10,000 miles, then had the brake pads and rotors replaced for a cost of $750. In this example, I drove the car another 10,000 miles and then repaired the brakes, the cost of which went from $1,100 to $750.

Unfortunately, some car dealers and repair shops will take advantage of the fact that most people have no idea what's wrong with their car and what it should cost. Going to someone you know is honest, reliable, and affordable will give you peace of mind and allow you to spend the money saved on other goals in your life.

How Do I Take Action?

How did I figure out that the guy I use to repair my cars was honest, reliable, and affordable? This takes a little trial and error. The first step is knowing that not all automobile dealers and repair shops are honest, and they don't charge the same amount for a specific repair.

When I move to a new area, I first ask my warm circle for recommendations. I will also look online at reviews. After that, I take my car to someone and ask a lot of questions.

How I absolutely knew I had my guy was when he told me to wait on replacing fuel injectors after another repair shop wanted to replace them. It was also confirmed several more times when he told me I could wait to have my brakes replaced.

I also compared his prices to competitors by calling and asking for pricing. For example, "How much do you charge for brake pads for my make, model, and year car?" Most dealers and repair shops will give you a price over the phone. You also need to ask for the type of brake pads they'll use. Premium brake pads use higher-quality materials. These materials typically have lower wear and therefore have a longer service life. You want to do this so you're comparing apples to apples.

Think about the calming effect of actually knowing you have someone you can trust to make the appropriate repairs, done correctly, and at a reasonable price. Doing this will save you money, stretch your earnings, and help you achieve your goals faster.

Chapter 5

Renting

Do you want to save money on your lease? Learn and understand what to do before you sign a lease on your apartment or home.

Action 19

I will carefully read and negotiate my lease.

Why Should I Take Action?

To help you understand the importance here, let me share three short stories. The first two are about people who just graduated from college, were entering the workforce full-time, and were signing their first apartment lease after college. The third story is about a couple in their late 20s and expecting their first baby.

The first story occurred when I was at a social gathering. One of the guests, Jay Walker, was excited about his first apartment after college and living in downtown Chicago. I asked him if he had negotiated his lease. His response to me was, "You can negotiate a lease?"

The second story is about Anita Job. who we learned about in Action 3. Like Jay, Anita had just graduated from college and was looking for an apartment in downtown Chicago. Anita found two apartments in the location she wanted where she could walk to work. She didn't want to buy a car because she was interested in saving money. She decided she could easily walk and use public transportation when needed. At this stage of her life, she wanted to spend her money elsewhere and not on a car that only depreciates.

During the walkthrough, Anita told the landlord that she had narrowed her search to two apartments and that the other apartment was $50 per month cheaper than this one. The landlord quickly said he would match the price and came down $50 per month. Anita saved $600 in her first year of renting an apartment outside of college. This may not seem like much, but it all adds up.

This $600 savings went to increase her 401(k), as Anita initially started her 401(k) with the minimum 5% to get the full employer match. After a few months of living on her own without her parents' help, and with her first full-time job, she realized she could afford to have 15% taken out of her paycheck. Increasing her 401(k) was one of her goals. Moving from 5% to 15% was possible, in part, because she saved $600 in rental payments.

Let's go back to the $600 savings from rent and think about how much that money will be worth with compound interest in 43 years. We learned the power of compound interest in Action 1. Investing $600 per year for 43 years with 10.12% interest will amount to $477,304.81. All Anita needed to do was negotiate her lease after reflecting on what was most important to her.

The last story is about Misty and Noah Rain. Misty and Noah were not interested in making a landlord rich. They were searching for a two-bedroom apartment because they were expecting their first child. They believed it could be their last year of renting an apartment in downtown Chicago as they were thinking about moving to a house in the suburbs to raise their family.

Misty went through one of the apartments with the landlord and really liked it. She told the landlord that she and her husband were expecting their first child. She indicated that she liked the apartment but it was $200 more than they wanted to spend. The landlord called her back the very next day and told her she would rent the apartment to Misty and Noah for $200 less than what she was asking. (On a side note, I feel pretty confident in saying that the landlord checked their credit and found they had wonderful credit, which helped get the rent lowered. This is yet another real-life example of the importance of establishing and maintaining good credit.)

The reality was that Noah and Misty actually could afford the

$200. However, they both believed in negotiating the rent so they could use the money elsewhere. Negotiating the rent saved them money, stretched their earnings, and helped them achieve their goals faster.

How Do I Take Action?

This is really quite simple. You have to ask. You can also use the same leverage that Anita and Misty used. These are true stories and they obviously worked for them. You can also propose a longer lease term like 18 months versus 12 months, which can drive down the rent. If you aren't good with negotiations, bring someone with you who is.

As we learned from the examples, this can save you money that you can use on other more important goals other than making your landlord rich. This represents opportunity cost. For Anita, saving money on her rent allowed her to increase her 401(k). This is a wonderful tradeoff just by initiating the conversation and seeing where it would go.

I can tell you from experience that landlords are more likely to come down on the monthly rent if you have really good credit. I've bought, rehabbed, and rented numerous properties with my brother, and we would lower the rental cost if someone who asked had really good credit. The peace of mind that we were renting to someone who more than likely was going to pay us on time every month was worth it to us. Landlords are also less likely to raise the rent if you pay them on time every month. Now go out and ASK! What do you have to lose?

Chapter 6

Buying a Home

Do you want to save tens of thousands of dollars in home ownership? Learn and understand the ins and outs of buying and selling your home.

Action 20

I will recognize the opportunity cost and value
in purchasing a home over renting.

Background Knowledge

When I use the terms buying or purchasing a home, I'm referring to a single-family home, condominium, townhome, or any structure that you actually own.

Equity – The value of your home minus how much you owe on your mortgage equals your home equity. Essentially, your equity is how much of the home you own versus how much the bank owns.

Home Appreciation – The increase of your home's value over time.

Principal – The amount you owe the bank on your mortgage. The principal starts out as the amount you originally borrowed and goes down after every monthly mortgage payment you make.

Why Should I Take Action?

I want you to recognize the opportunity cost and value in purchasing a home over renting. To do this, we will explore two important concepts. Both concepts involve building wealth through real estate. The first concept has to do with equity. Every time you make a monthly mortgage payment, a portion of that payment brings down your principal and raises your equity. In other words, you own more of your home and you owe less to the bank after every single monthly mortgage payment.

In contrast, every time you make your monthly rent payment, you're only helping your landlord. You never get anything back financially from making rent payments after you move out. While this is wonderful for the landlord, over long periods, this can add up to a significant amount of money that you'll never get back. When you own the home you're living in, you can get your equity back from making monthly payments when you sell the home.

The second important concept I want you to recognize in this action statement is home appreciation. During normal times, homes in good neighborhoods will go up in value. In fact, according to the Federal Housing Finance Agency (FHFA), from 2000 to 2022, the average annual home appreciation rate has been 4.7%.[15] FHFA is considered a good measure of historical appreciation by experts in the field. Please recognize home appreciation can vary from state to state, city to city, and even within each city or town.

Let's look at an example using this historical 4.7% annual appreciation rate to recognize the importance of this concept. In Figure 6-1, we look at the appreciation of a home we purchased for $250,000.

In Figure 6-1, we see that our home appreciated by $145,737 over 10 years. In essence, we are worth $145,737 more by owning our home rather than renting. I purposely kept the example simple to make it easy to understand the concept. This example doesn't include other variables such as maintenance costs or the cost of selling our home. However, after reading this action statement, you should be able to recognize the opportunity cost and value in gaining equity through monthly mortgage payments and appreciation. This is a direct result of purchasing a home over renting a home. Essentially, you are building wealth through real estate when you own your home as opposed to renting.

Figure 6-1

Year	Home Value
End of Year 1	$261,750
End of Year 2	$274,052
End of Year 3	$286,933
End of Year 4	$300,419
End of Year 5	$314,538
End of Year 6	$329,322
End of Year 7	$344,800
End of Year 8	$361,005
End of Year 9	$377,972
End of Year 10	$395,737

How Do I Take Action?

After I graduated from college, I rented for one year before I bought my first home. I never wanted to make a landlord rich. In fact, my brother and I decided to buy several homes and rent them out so we could make money from other people and build wealth through real estate.

Please note that I'm not suggesting you should buy a home over renting. This action statement is written to say, "Recognize the opportunity cost and value in purchasing a home over renting." I grew up in the suburbs of Chicago. Many of my friends as well as my nieces and nephews wanted to live in Chicago after graduating from college and experience the big-city life. They weren't interested in purchasing a home right away so they ended up renting apartments for many years.

I chose to purchase a home over renting because of the financial ramifications. However, there are additional factors you should consider before making this decision. There are numerous advantages to renting, including a lifestyle with no maintenance, access to amenities (pool, fitness center), and more flexibility, to name a few. Other factors to consider when choosing a place to live include your age, work situation, desired location, and readiness to settle down for the long haul. It's much easier to move when you're renting as you don't have to sell your home to move to a new location.

My goal with this action statement is to make you aware of the opportunity cost and value (financial ramifications) that you'll miss out on should you decide to rent. Now that you understand the opportunity costs of buying and renting, you need to decide how you (and your family) want to live now and in the future.

Action 21

I will save enough money for a down payment
on a home so I can avoid or reduce
PMI (Private Mortgage Insurance).

Background Knowledge

In Action 20, we learned how we could build wealth by owning a home instead of renting. We also learned numerous factors that go into our decision to buy or rent. Action 21 is written for those who decide to first rent before buying a home. I'm encouraging you to save money for a down payment on a future home while you're renting.

Private Mortgage Insurance (PMI) – PMI is required when your down payment on a home is less than 20%. For example, if you're purchasing a $250,000 home, you'll need to put down $50,000 to avoid the PMI expense. The insurance protects the lender (not you) if you default or can't make payments on your home loan.

PMI typically costs between 0.22% and 2.25% of your mortgage. Two main factors that determine what percentage you'll pay are how much you're borrowing (larger loans pay more) and your credit score. The higher your credit score, the lower your PMI percentage. Your lender is required by law to have you stop paying PMI once you've paid 22% of your mortgage.

Why Should I Take Action?

PMI increases the cost of your home loan. The most common way to pay for PMI is through a monthly premium that's added to your mortgage payment. If you put less than 20% down on your home, you'll be required to purchase PMI. If you get a loan with less than 20% down and the lender doesn't make you purchase PMI, they'll make you pay a higher interest rate. Either way, you lose out because you have to pay more for the cost of the home loan.

Let's look at an example in which we purchase a $250,000 home and put 5% down or $12,500. The example includes credit scores of 640 and 740 so we can once again see the importance of establishing and maintaining a good credit score (Action 9).

Figure 6-2

	640 Credit Score	740 Credit Score	Difference
PMI Cost Factor	.85%	.29%	
Monthly Amount	$168.23	$57.40	
Duration	11 Years	11 Years	
Total PMI Cost	$20,662.56	$7,362.96	$13,299.60
Total in 5 Years	$10,093.80	$3,444.00	$6,649.80

In this simple but realistic example, you can see how your credit score plays a significant role in how much you pay for PMI. You also learn how expensive PMI is, as in this example, the cost is $20,662.56 for someone with a 640 credit score and $7,362.96 for someone with a 740 credit score. That's a whole lot of extra money.

This is why, if you choose to initially rent, saving enough money for a 20% down payment on your home can save you thousands of dollars, stretch your earnings, and help you achieve your goals faster.

How Do I Take Action?

This will need to be a goal of yours. To illustrate, let me share two stories that have very different circumstances. The first true story is from one of my nephews, who I called Jack Indabox in Action 4. Jack understood the financial ramifications when he chose to rent over buying a home. He wanted to rent because he wasn't ready to settle down yet and enjoyed the lifestyle that renting in the city provided him.

Because he initially chose to rent for several years and forgo the wealth building that comes with home ownership, Jack made one of his goals in life to save enough money so he wouldn't have to pay PMI when the time came to purchase his first home. As a result, he started a home down-payment fund. He started this when he was single and continued when he was first married. Jack wanted to rent in downtown Chicago and then one day buy a home in the suburbs after having children.

Jack first maxed out his 401(k), and as he continued to get raises, he didn't raise his cost of living. Instead, he took the extra income and started his home down-payment fund. He made the conscious decision to start the fund because he knew in the long run, PMI would cost him more money. Let me share Jack's thought process:

> "Housing is a basic necessity that, for the most part, eats up the largest portion of our monthly budget and likely will be the largest purchase in life. As such, I wanted

to ensure I took the necessary steps well before being in the market to be able to purchase a home on my desired timeline with financial confidence.

"I knew I was not immediately ready or interested in buying a home but would likely want to purchase something in the next several years. It felt like a purchase several years from now was a tomorrow problem, but I kept thinking how it would be the largest purchase of my life. As such, I reached out to my bank and set up a separate savings account (housing account). I then contributed a monthly amount of my savings to the housing account on the first day of every month. Over the next several years, the housing account continued to grow and put me in a position to be able to buy a home on my terms (not when I had enough saved up). The housing account also will allow me to avoid PMI with a 20% down payment and make me feel confident with the future mortgage obligation."

In this true story, Jack simply made it a goal of his and took the necessary steps to make it happen. This included the conscious decision to keep his standard of living the same after earning his annual pay increases.

Let's look at a second example with very different life circumstances. This is also a true story that comes from a different nephew, who we'll call Willie Bethere. Willie began his career right out of college working for a company in his hometown. He really enjoyed working for this company. At the time, he knew he wanted to marry his high school sweetheart and stay in town both to work and live.

Willie wasn't interested in making a landlord rich, so he wanted to purchase a starter home as soon as possible. He bought his first home at age 23. However, because he had just started his first full-time job, he didn't have enough money to put 20% down to avoid the PMI.

This was really an annoyance to him because he understood PMI was essentially throwing his hard-earned money away. However, he also recognized that paying PMI was better than making rent payments to a landlord. After he closed on the house, he made the conscious decision to pay as much extra as he could every month (Action 25) to pay down the loan, which would allow him to get rid of the PMI payment. After two years, he was able to refinance (Action 24) the loan to a shorter term, going from a 30-year to a 15-year loan (Action 23). During the refinance, he had the house appraised, and between the extra payments and the house appraising higher (meaning that it went up in value), he had the 25% equity he needed to get rid of the PMI.

Now instead of paying for PMI, Willie could put more money in his pocket. He continued to pay extra on his monthly mortgage after the PMI was removed to limit the amount of interest he would pay. Continuing to do this greatly helped him in the long run. When he eventually sold this home, he had enough money to put 20% down on his next home and avoid PMI altogether.

This true story has a happy ending because he did marry his high school sweetheart, and they had three children in this second home. Willie says, "In my opinion, PMI is just a wasted expense that I wanted to avoid at all cost or at least pay as little of it as possible, so I had a plan and followed that plan to get rid of it."

These are two very different stories, and hopefully, you can relate to one of them. However, two variables are the same in both stories. First, both Jack and Willie understood PMI should be avoided when possible, and they made it a goal of theirs to eliminate it. Second, they both kept their standard of living the same as they received annual raises and took the extra money to conquer PMI. Why did they do this? Because it allowed them to save money, stretch their earnings, and achieve their goals faster.

I want to make sure I'm very clear with Action 20 and Action 21. I did not wait until I had 20% equity to buy a home, nor would I recommend that you do so. In normal times, you will more than make up for what you pay in PMI by building wealth through equity accumulation in real estate. However, if you decide you want to rent for whatever reason, make it a goal to save money for a down payment to avoid PMI when you do decide you are ready to buy a home and settle down.

Action 22

I will cancel my PMI when I have enough equity.

Why Should I Take Action?

We learned in Action 21 that PMI is an added expense. Most people continue to pay PMI month after month and forget that they're even paying for it. There's an old saying that says, "Out of sight, out of mind." They don't realize they can typically stop paying PMI after they gain enough equity in their home.

Equity happens when the value of your home goes up, and it also happens when you make monthly mortgage payments. Each time you make a payment, the amount of equity you have goes up. In other words, how much of the home you own goes up and how much of the home the bank owns goes down with each payment you make.

Why should you take action? I think a better question is why wouldn't you want to take action?

Why would you want to keep making monthly PMI payments to the bank when the money has absolutely no benefit to you?

Do you think you would have a better place for this dollar amount that you pay every month?

Think of the opportunity cost. In the realistic example we already looked at in Figure 6-2, we see that PMI costs $168.23 per month for someone with a 640 credit score. You can continue to pay this amount month after month and year after year or you can cancel it and use the money on one of your other goals in life. This saves you money, stretches your earnings, and helps you achieve your goals faster.

How Do I Take Action?

We learned that you'll need to purchase PMI when the down payment on your home is less than 20%. However, banks won't let you cancel PMI at 20% equity. They'll let you cancel at 22% or 25% equity. Why the difference?

If you solely use your monthly payments in determining your equity, you can typically cancel PMI insurance at 22% equity. If you're basing the equity both on your monthly payments and the fact that your house has gone up in value, which is called appreciation, you can typically cancel at 25% equity.

During normal housing markets, you can count on an average of 3% to 4% per year increase in your home value. There are a lot of other variables that go into this appreciation percentage, such as neighborhood, city, and state. For example, you may live in an area that has higher real estate appreciation because it's a "hot area" or you may live in an area that has lower appreciation because it's a less desirable area.

In Figure 6-3, we look at how quickly you can gain the 25% equity needed to cancel your PMI. In this example, we look at purchasing a $250,000 home with a 30-year fixed-rate mortgage with a 5% down payment and a 4% appreciation rate.

In this simple example, we were able to gain 25% equity in four years. When you reach 25% equity in your home, request PMI cancellation in writing to your lender. You can go to a website like Zillow to figure out how much your home is worth or you can call your realtor and ask them for the current market value of your home. Most realtors won't charge you anything for this help as they hope when you go to sell your home one day that you'll list your home with them. If you find out you have 25% equity, write that letter to your lender.

Figure 6-3

	4 Percent Appreciation	Mortgage Balance	Percentage Equity
Purchased Value	$250,000	$237,500	5%
End of Year One Value	$261,070	$233,996	10%
End of Year Two Value	$271,513	$230,312	15%
End of Year Three Value	$282,374	$226,441	20%
End of Year Four Value	$293,669	$222,371	25%

Going back to Action 21 and analyzing Figure 6-2, we see that canceling PMI after five years with a 640 credit score can save us $10,568.76. Paying that is a complete waste of money when all we need to do is let our lender know we have 25% equity in our home. Note that in Figure 6-3, we did not include the reality that your equity will go up even more from making monthly payments. Making payments will help you gain equity faster and save you even more money.

Be aware that if you make a late payment on your mortgage, the lender is not obligated to cancel your PMI. Hopefully, you learned the importance of a good credit score (Action 9), which also allows you to cancel PMI when you gain 25% equity.

Action 23

I will choose the right mortgage
for my circumstances.

Background Knowledge

Pre-Qualified Mortgage – Most realtors will make you get pre-qualified before they walk you through any homes. Essentially, getting pre-qualified gives you and your realtor an estimate of what you may be able to borrow based on your financial data and credit check. This allows realtors to show you homes you can afford.

Fixed-Rate Mortgage – The interest rate remains the same for the length of the loan. Typical fixed-rate loans include 30-year and 15-year loans.

Adjustable-Rate Mortgage (ARM) – The interest rate adjusts over time based on the market. Whether the rate goes up or down depends on what the Federal Reserve does with interest rates (Action Statement 12). ARMs may offer a lower initial interest rate than a fixed rate.

Why Should I Take Action?

Take a look at Figure 6-4, which shows a $250,000 fixed-rate mortgage with a 4% interest rate. The first column of numbers represents a 30-year fixed-rate loan, and the second column of numbers represents a 15-year fixed-rate loan.

Figure 6-4 ($250,000 Loan)

	30-Year Fixed	15-Year Fixed
Monthly Payment	$1,193.54	$1,849.22
How much of your payment goes to interest on the first payment?	$833.33	$833.33
How much of your payment goes to interest on the last payment?	$3.97	$6.14
How much do you owe after one year of making payments?	$245,597.41	$237,583.37
How much interest will you pay the bank over the life of the loan?	$179,673.77	$82,859.57

You can learn at least four important concepts from the example in Figure 6-4.

1. You pay a lot of interest to a bank for your mortgage.
2. Most of the interest is paid upfront on your mortgage.
3. The difference in interest between a 30-year and a 15-year fixed-rate mortgage in this example is $96,814.20. That's a very large number and makes a huge difference.
4. Your monthly payment is $655.68 more per month to have a 15-year over a 30-year fixed-rate mortgage.

I believe you can arrive at a fairly straightforward conclusion from this typical example. If you can afford the monthly payment on a 15-year fixed-rate mortgage, you should choose this option over a 30-year fixed-rate mortgage. Why? In our simple example, I can give you $96,814.20 reasons. Can you think of the opportunity cost of saving $96,814.20 in interest to a bank? Do you think this stretches your earnings and achieves your goals faster? Do you think you could find other places to spend $96,814.20?

In Figure 6-5 we use the same interest rate. However, what makes a 15-year mortgage even more enticing is the interest rate is typically lower than a 30-year mortgage. To illustrate, my mortgage broker quoted a 30-year mortgage at 6.5% and a 15-year mortgage at 5.625% on a $250,000 loan.

Figure 6-5

	15-Year Fixed-Rate Mortgage at 5.625%	30-Year Fixed-Rate Mortgage at 6.5%
Monthly Payment	$2,059.33	$1,580.17
Total Interest Paid	$120,679.27	$318,861.22

Looking at the numbers in Figure 6-5, which mortgage is best for your situation? If you choose the 15-year mortgage, you have a much higher monthly payment, but you pay $198,181 less in overall interest to a bank. If you don't qualify or can't afford the monthly payments on the 15-year fixed-rate mortgage, the decision is an easier one. However, if you do qualify and can afford the payments on the 15-year fixed-rate mortgage, you'll save a significant amount of money in interest to a bank. Choosing the right mortgage for your situation is important because your home is typically the most expensive purchase you'll make in your life. Take the time to compare, analyze the numbers, and make an informed decision that makes the most sense for your circumstances.

How Do I Take Action?

Most if not all realtors will have you call a loan officer to get pre-qualified before walking you through homes for sale. Don't worry, as they have relationships with many loan officers and they'll recommend someone for you.

When you get pre-qualified with a loan officer, they'll ask you all sorts of questions about your finances, including what your gross income is, how much your car payment is, how much credit card debt you have (I hope you tell them "none," as you should pay your credit cards off in full every month), how long you've worked at your current employer, and more. They'll also run a credit check on you (Action 9).

Based on the information gathered, they'll write a pre-qualification letter sharing how much money you'll be able to borrow. With that information, you now know what price range of homes you can start to look at with your realtor.

It's important to point out that just because you qualify for higher-priced homes doesn't mean you should go out and borrow that much money. Remember, if you decide to borrow the maximum amount, the opportunity cost is less money to do other things in your life. Go back to your goals (Action 7) and put into perspective the largest purchase and ultimately the largest expense you probably will encounter throughout life.

When I met with my loan officer, I asked him to tell me how much I could borrow on a 15-year fixed-rate mortgage as well as a 30-year fixed-rate mortgage. Because the monthly payment is higher on a 15-year loan, you won't be able to borrow as much money. However, the interest rate will be lower, which also has an effect on how much you can borrow. As a result, the price range of houses you can afford will go down for a 15-year loan. We will typically purchase two to four homes in our lifetimes. Many people buy a smaller, less expensive starter home and then move to a bigger home later in life. Each time I looked to move, I had my loan officer share how much I could afford with a 15-year versus a 30-year loan.

Because I couldn't afford much with my first home, I went with a 30-year loan. This wasn't much of a home to begin with, and I needed the lower monthly payments. However, after my wife and I both received annual raises, we eventually went with a 15-year mortgage to save a boatload of interest. I'm not saying you can't take out a 30-year mortgage. I'm saying you should be educated and knowledgeable about both options so you can make an informed decision.

The price range of the home we qualified for using a 15-year mortgage was enough home for us. In other words, we didn't need a larger, more expensive home. As a result, we used the money we would have paid to a bank on a 30-year mortgage for interest on our other goals in life like maxing out our 401(k) and traveling. This ultimately saved us money and stretched our earnings.

There are also adjustable-rate mortgages. These mortgages have a fixed rate for a set period and then adjust up or down accordingly. For example, common ARMs include 5/1 and 7/1. The 5/1 would have a fixed interest rate for the first five years and then adjust up or down from there. In the past, banks would entice borrowers with lower interest rates on ARMs compared to the fixed rate. I took advantage of this lower interest rate as my gut told me we would move in less than five years, which is what happened. This saved me money in interest because the ARM had a lower interest rate than the fixed-rate mortgage.

In general, banks don't offer the favorable rates they once did on ARM loans. As a result, these typically will not be a good option for you, however, I wanted to share ARMs with you in case this changes in the future. Your mortgage broker can let you know if these are a viable option. To that end, when you ask your mortgage broker to quote how much you can afford on a 15-year and a 30-year fixed-rate loan, also inquire about other loans such as ARMs. Doing this will let you be informed so you can choose the right mortgage for your situation.

Action 24

I will appropriately take advantage of lower
interest rates and refinance my mortgage.

Background Knowledge
Refinance – Taking out a new loan at a lower interest rate and
using that money to pay off the older higher interest rate loan.

Why Should I Take Action?
You have to hear the story of Bill Overdue. Bill bought a home
in 2018, borrowing $250,000 on a 30-year fixed-rate mort-
gage at 4.54% interest. Bill refinanced his existing 4.54% loan in
February of 2021 with an interest rate of 2.81%. At this time, Bill
still owed $237,420.70 on his mortgage.

Figure 6-6

Interest Rate	Monthly Payment	Total Interest Paid (30 years)
4.54%	$1,272.66	$208,158.31
2.81%	$976.81	$114,231.30

In this example, with actual interest rates at the time, Bill was
able to refinance his existing mortgage and lower his monthly payment by $295.85. Think about how nice it would be to free up
$295.85 every single month. Bill will also save over $93,000 in total
interest on his loan as a result of the refinance.

Why should you refinance your mortgage when interest rates
go down? This example frees up $295.85 per month and saves you

over $93,000 in interest payments to a bank. Of course you want to take advantage of lower interest rates.

How Do I Take Action?

In Action 12, we looked at the importance of knowing what the Federal Reserve is doing with interest rates. We come full circle with this action statement as we see firsthand how important it is to be aware of what's going on with interest rates. Being informed can help you refinance at the appropriate time when interest rates are low, and maybe if you do the appropriate research, you will refinance when interest rates are at the lowest point they'll be for a while. Doing this will allow you to take advantage of a lower monthly payment as well as savings on the total amount of interest paid to a bank.

You may also be able to refinance your existing mortgage and move from a 30-year to a 15-year fixed-rate mortgage at the same time (Action 23). This is twice as nice because you refinance to a lower interest rate along with a shorter loan period. This can save you even more money in interest payments to a bank.

One last point you need to know to implement this action statement is that refinancing is not free. Banks let you refinance at a lower interest rate, but they'll also charge you a loan origination fee to do it. As you can imagine, this amount is different from bank to bank.

One of the questions you should ask when looking to refinance, besides the interest rates on 30-year and 15-year fixed-rate loans, is how much refinancing will cost, specifically the loan origination fee. Just so you have a frame of reference, the cost to refinance may be around $2,500. Due to various taxes and government fees, this can vary from state to state. You don't need to pay this amount in cash if you don't have it. Rather, you can roll this amount into the new home loan.

However, it's important to remember Action 12: "I will look at what the Federal Reserve is doing with interest rates before buying a home or car." We can change this action statement for our purposes here to say, "It is important to look at what the Federal Reserve is doing with interest rates before refinancing." Why? Because you don't want to refinance only to have the interest rates go down even lower the next month.

I have a friend who has been a mortgage broker for over 35 years, and he refinanced a guy three times in one year. The customer kept calling him to refinance when they realized interest rates were continuing to go down.

A little research could have saved this customer thousands of dollars in refinancing fees. Remember the Federal Reserve doesn't typically make knee-jerk reactions. In other words, this person easily could have learned that the Fed was considering lowering interest rates even further.

Another customer refinanced the same home seven times. I don't blame my friend as it's not a mortgage broker's job to predict when interest rates will be at their lowest. Rather, it's our job as educated and informed consumers.

As we learned in Action 12, this is fairly easy to do. Knowing what the Federal Reserve is doing with interest rates is important so you don't waste the cost of refinancing several times.

Don't let the cost of the refinance stop you from refinancing. Your mortgage broker can let you know how long it will take you to recapture the cost of refinancing, how much you'll be saving per month, and how much you'll save in interest over the life of the loan. As you can see from our examples, refinancing when interest rates are lower will save you money, stretch your earnings, and help you achieve your goals faster.

Action 25

I will consider making extra
payments on my mortgage.

Background Knowledge

When you make your mortgage payment every month, you
can add more money to the payment. For example, if your
payment is $1,100 per month, you can pay $1,150 per month. This
would be $50 extra per month. The extra amount doesn't need to
be the same every month. You can pay $50 one month, $10 another
month, and $200 a third month. This extra amount goes to
pay down the principal on the loan and doesn't go toward the interest
on the loan.

Why Should I Take Action?

Let's pound this point home by looking at a couple of examples.
In Figure 6-7, we look at a $250,000, 30-year fixed-rate
loan with a 7.76% interest rate. The industry source for mortgage
rates is Freddie Mac, and between April 1971 and March 2024, 30-year
fixed-rate mortgages averaged 7.74%.[16]

Figure 6-7

Extra Monthly Payment	Total Interest Saved	Mortgage Shortened
$50 more per month	$45,361	2 years 10 months
$100 more per month	$79,746	5 years 1 month
$250 more per month	$148,051	9 years 8 months

We learn in Figure 6-7 that paying an extra $100 per month can save $80,117.98 in interest payments to a bank. This is a lot of money that can be used toward one of your other goals in life. You'll also shorten the 30-year loan by five years and one month.

In our second example, we'll change only the interest rate as we look at a $250,000 30-year fixed-rate loan with a 4% interest rate.

Figure 6-8

Extra Monthly Payment	Total Interest Saved	Mortgage Shortened
$50 more per month	$15,236.90	2 years 2 months
$100 more per month	$27,957.35	4 years 1 month
$250 more per month	$56,161.27	8 years 5 months

You can find an online mortgage calculator to plug in your own loan numbers to determine what you could save by making extra payments every month. I loved looking at this when I was younger with a mortgage just to see how much I could save. This motivated me to pay as much extra as possible, which led to paying off my mortgage a lot quicker. The moral of the story here is paying extra on your mortgage every month can save you a boatload in interest to a bank.

How Do I Take Action?

Typically, you and your significant other will get annual raises from your employer. If you keep your standard of living similar, you will have more money per month in discretionary income. You can use this money in many ways.

One option is to take some of the extra discretionary income and add money to your mortgage payment. As you can see from Figures 6-7 and 6-8, this will save you a substantial amount of money in interest. However, I would only do this if you've maxed out your 401(k) first. I say this because, in most years, you'll make more money in interest in your 401(k) than the interest rate you pay on your mortgage.

I use the word "consider" in the action statement because there is another option to consider. You can take the extra discretionary income and invest it. Strictly from a financial point of view, this is a better option as most years you'll make more money than you would save on your mortgage.

In full disclosure, my wife and I regularly made extra payments to our mortgages throughout our lives. Many of these loans (we have had several houses) had low-interest rates. I totally understood at the time that we would have been better off financially by investing the extra money.

However, there's something to be said for the peace of mind we received from owning our home free and clear without a loan from a bank. I also felt comfort in knowing that if something happened to me, my wife, who doesn't show as much interest in our finances and as such relies on me to take care of them, would not have to worry about a mortgage. This brought both of us a sense of comfort, and it was worth it.

Now that I laid out both options for you, you need to decide which option is best for you and your family. Please remember I'm giving you two options, and keeping up with the Joneses isn't one of them. Both options take your discretionary income and stretch the money to help you achieve your goals faster.

Action 26

I will negotiate real estate commissions
when selling my home.

Background Knowledge

Note: As of this publication, the National Association of Realtors has settled its commission lawsuits and will have to make changes to decades-long policies on real estate agent commissions. The good news from the settlement is that commissions will now be more transparent, which should make it easier for you to negotiate. While I don't have a crystal ball, I will state current practices as well as likely changes throughout Action 26.

When you sell your home with a typical realtor, you'll pay a commission to list your home and a commission to sell your home. For example, you may have a 3% listing commission and a 3% selling commission for a total of 6%. If you were listing and selling a $250,000 home, your real estate commission would be $7,500 paid to the realtor who listed your home and $7,500 to the realtor who sold your home. This would mean $15,000 from the sale of your home is not going back to you. You don't pay for either unless your home sells.

There's no standard split between the listing agent and the selling agent. The split could be 50/50 or 60/40 or a different percentage. The percentages are determined when you list your home with a realtor and are written into the listing contract. One thing to point out about the current real estate commission system is that it's not an experience- or performance-based commission system.

In other words, someone who's been a realtor for one week and knows very little about the industry will make the same commission as an experienced realtor who's been doing it for 30 years. This may be one of the changes from the lawsuits, as experienced realtors may charge more than inexperienced realtors.

Additionally, many people think the buyer pays their real estate agent when they buy a home. In fact, while the buyer brings the money to closing to buy the home, the money to pay both the listing agent and the buying agent comes out of the proceeds from the seller. This may change in the future.

Why Should I Take Action?

The money you pay in real estate commissions is typically the largest expense you'll have when you sell your home. In 2022, the average homeowner across the United States spent $19,214 on realtor commissions. This represents a significant amount of money taken out of the profits from the sale of your home.[17]

However, real estate commissions are not set in stone. Just as rents are negotiable, real estate commissions are also negotiable. You can always negotiate realtor commissions with your realtor or sell with a discount real estate broker (more on this later).

Commissions across the United States averaged between 4.45% and 6.34% (this includes both listing and selling your home).[17] Let's look at the high and low end of the average when we sell our home for $250,000.

We would save $4,725 in commissions going from the high end of the average to the low end. Do you think you could find somewhere else to spend that $4,725? To save this money, you will need to negotiate the realtor sales commission.

Figure 6-9

Commission Percentage	Commission Amount
4.45%	$11,125
6.34%	$15,850

Another option is to list your home with a discount real estate broker. These agents work for companies that have a different business model. You can do a Google search for discount real estate brokers in your area. These companies will typically list your home for either a flat fee like $350 or for a discounted percentage like 1% or 1.5% compared to a more typical 2.5% or 3%.

They'll offer a free consultation to help you decide on the commission for the buyer's agent (the agent that sells your home). This could include market time (how long it will take to sell your home) based on the commission percentage. The theory here is the lower the commission percentage, the longer it will take to sell your home.

Some realtors won't actively show your home to potential clients if the commission is lower than a more typical 2.5% or 3%. This means fewer people going through your home, which could mean a longer time to sell it. However, because homes are listed online, potential buyers still can see a home they like and ask their realtor to see it. This was different when homes were not listed electronically on the Multiple Listing Service (MLS) for everyone to see. You can now go to MLS.com to find real estate listings for sale by realtors.

However, in a hot market where you might receive multiple offers the same day your home is listed, the percentage can be lower and you'll still sell your home quickly. You'll need to decide in a down market if a lower buyer's agent commission is worth it because it may affect how long it takes to sell your home.

In Figure 6-10 we look at the difference between going with a discount real estate broker with a listing of 1.5% and paying the buyer's agent 2.5% for a total of 4% compared to a more traditional 5% or 6%. This is based on selling the home for $250,000.

Figure 6-10

Commission Percentage	Commission Amount
4%	$10,000
5%	$12,500
6%	$15,000

In this example, you can save $2,500 to $5,000 by listing your home with a discount real estate broker. In summary, you can either negotiate your real estate commission with a traditional agent or list your home with a discount real estate broker. Both options will save you money, stretch your earnings, and help you achieve your goals faster.

How Do I Take Action?

You have two distinct options here. First, you can perform a Google search in your area and talk to discount real estate brokers. Make sure you look at their reviews. It's important to note with discount realtors that the lower the fee or percentage, the less they will actually do to sell your home. However, your home will be listed on the MLS website for all realtors and potential buyers to see. In a hot market, this can be all you need to sell your home.

Another option is to negotiate with a traditional real estate agent. I've found most real estate agents will come down very quickly from 6% to 5%. I've also found that some will come down to 4.5%. It's more challenging to negotiate something lower with a traditional real estate agent. This ultimately will depend on numerous outside factors beyond your control. One such factor is whether the market is hot or slow.

Based on the lawsuits, one of the changes could be realtors coming down even lower than 6%, 5%, or even 4.5%. This will make negotiations even more worthwhile in the future

I wouldn't list with someone for 6%. Why would I when there are plenty of really good realtors who'll do it for less? The bottom line here is: As you learned in some of the other action items, you have to negotiate. This simply starts by posing the question to your realtor, or many realtors, if you don't have one yet.

It's also important to recognize a down market. In times like these, your realtor may rightfully inform you that they'll need to spend more money than usual to sell your home. They may want to have an open house several times a month and have drone pictures taken of your property, along with other services that will help sell your home in a down market. If the cost of their services goes up, so will their desire (rightfully so) to charge you more for those services.

Besides the commission, you also want to make sure you're working with someone you enjoy being around. While you're not looking for a new best friend, you'll typically spend enough time with this person to where you want to enjoy their personality. My wife and I knew fairly quickly if it was a match or not, and I'm sure you'll know as well. Hopefully, you can find someone you can work with for all or most of your home purchases throughout your life.

I've bought and sold numerous homes in my life. Some I lived in and some I rented out. I've primarily worked with two realtors from different areas over the last 35 years. I enjoy their company and trust them. This is an important consideration along with the commission we discussed earlier. When it's time to sell your home, find a realtor you enjoy working with who's either a traditional realtor or a discount realtor, and negotiate the commission. This will save you money, stretch your earnings, and help you achieve your goals faster.

Chapter 7

Insurance

Do you want comfort and peace of mind knowing you have the necessary insurance protection for the least amount of money? Learn and understand the ins and outs of auto, home, health, life and renters insurance.

Action 27

I will shop around for insurance.

Background Knowledge

Insurance – An arrangement in which a company provides compensation for specified loss, damage, illness, or death in exchange for the payment of a premium. Insurance offers us protection or a safety net.

Premium – The amount you pay for insurance coverage.

Deductible – The amount you pay on a claim before an insurance provider will pay any expenses.

Claim – A request for payment after you experience a loss. If your car is damaged in an accident, you'll file a claim to begin the process with the insurance company to pay for the repairs.

Policy – A contract document that details the terms and conditions between the insurance company and the policyholder.

Insurance Agent – Someone who sells insurance from a single provider like State Farm or Allstate.

Insurance Broker – Someone who sells insurance from multiple insurance companies. This typically will range from three to more than 20 companies.

Why Should I Take Action?

My brother, who we'll call Jim Nasium, has been an insurance broker for more than 25 years, and I've purposely learned a lot from him on how to save money with my various insurance policies. Insurance is not a luxury but a necessity. We need auto, health, home, and life insurance protection. As a result, I continually ask how I can have great coverage while paying the least amount of money.

One of the best ways to save money is by shopping around for your insurance. Insurance companies can charge substantially different rates. A good question to ask is: Why do insurance companies charge substantially different rates?

One big reason for price variations is that insurance companies have decades of claim statistics that ultimately affect the rates they charge. For example, one company may have a horrible claim history with drivers over 70 years old and another company may not have had many claims until their customers are in their 80s. The first company will not have very good rates for people in their 70s, while the second company will have better rates. Previous claims on older drivers, younger drivers, good credit scores, bad credit scores, old homes, and new homes along with many other criteria will all affect the price various insurance companies charge.

I asked Jim Nasium for an example with actual numbers, and he quoted a homeowners policy where the customer was paying $1,894. My brother was able to offer the same coverage for $937. This is a $957 annual savings. Think about paying this higher amount over the next 40 or 50 years. That's a whole lot of extra money paid for the same coverage. Quite frankly, it's a waste of your hard-earned money.

You can continue to pay the higher premium year after year or you can shop around to get the best rate and use the savings on one of your other goals in life. The money you save by shopping around stretches your earnings and helps you achieve your goals faster.

How Do I Take Action?

Call a handful of insurance companies in your area to get comparable quotes. Make sure you're comparing apples to apples. For example, for auto insurance, you should compare the same coverage limits (Action 31) and deductibles (Action 29).

When I move to a new area, I also like to ask my warm circle for agents and companies they recommend. There's nothing better than getting recommendations from your warm circle. You can also do a Google search to find reviews on insurance agents near you.

Once you get different quotes, compare them to make sure the companies are quoting the same coverage, and then choose the agent and company you want to work with. Auto and home insurance will be for the year, and life insurance may be a longer term like 10 or 20 years (Action 38).

Make sure to also get a quote from an insurance broker. A broker represents multiple insurance companies, and they can get a quote for you from all of the insurance providers they work with. Essentially, this is one-stop shopping. As we learned earlier, insurance companies vary in price, and a broker who represents 20 insurance companies can quickly help you determine which company they represent has the best price for you. A broker typically represents companies that don't advertise on television, so don't be afraid if you've never heard of the company. Think about it. One reason you may be able to get a lower premium is the fact they don't spend a bunch of money on TV advertising. I've obviously used a broker most of my life (my brother) and never had any trouble with these less well-known companies.

One of the main advantages of working with a broker is the ability to check pricing with numerous insurance companies while working with one person. A broker may also allow you to work with the same agent throughout your life because of their ability to use different companies based on your circumstances. As your circumstances or criteria change, so may the company that offers the best rate based on these changing circumstances.

It should be noted that you probably don't want to be switching insurance companies for minimal amounts. The amount of time you stay with an insurance company can affect your rates. Some companies use risk scores. Two factors that go into risk scores include how long you've been with your carrier and how many carriers you've had in the last five years. You also don't want to switch insurance companies for minimal amounts if your agent and company have been responsive and given you good customer service.

However, make sure you do the initial shopping around and check your rates every three or four years. You should also check your rates when you have a change in your circumstances, such as adding a 16-year-old child to your auto policy. This will save you money, stretch your earnings, and help you reach your goals faster. Why throw money out the window for the exact same coverage when all you need to do is shop around?

Action 28

I will take advantage of insurance discounts.

Background Knowledge

Bundling – Discount offered to customers who purchase several types of insurance from the same company, such as bundling your auto and home insurance.

Why Should I Take Action?

Insurance companies offer different types of discounts. Some examples include good credit, multi-car discounts, low-mileage discounts, paperless discounts, paid-in-full discounts, home security discounts, longevity discounts, no-claim discounts, and bundling discounts.

For example, I get a $573 discount for bundling my auto and home insurance policies. I also get a $42 discount for paying my premium in full every year as well as a $163 discount for not filing a claim on my home policy.

This is $778 per year in insurance discounts on my auto and home insurance. I also get a good credit discount, which we'll talk more about in Action 30. While insurance is a necessity, how much we pay is a very large variable. You need to take advantage of the discounts offered on your various insurance policies to stretch your earnings and use this money to help pay for other goals in life.

How Do I Take Action?

The first step is to be aware that insurance companies offer numerous discounts. The next step is to inquire about the discounts. Don't assume the insurance agent will automatically offer you a discount. Ask them about the discounts discussed here, and also ask if there are any other discounts their company offers. All you have to do is ask, and you can save a whole lot of money every year. Now is not the time to be shy or quiet. TAKE ACTION! Ask your insurance agent.

Action 29

I will consider my deductibles when
purchasing auto and home insurance.

Why Should I Take Action?

As we learned earlier in Action 27, a deductible is the amount you pay before an insurance provider pays any expenses on a claim. For example, if you get into an accident and file a claim, the deductible is the amount you'll have to pay before the insurance company starts to pay their share of the claim.

There is an inverse relationship between deductibles and premiums. In other words, the higher the deductible, the lower the premium, and the lower the deductible. the higher the premium.

In Figure 7-1, we look at an auto policy for a 2021 GMC Sierra pickup truck for a 27-year-old. This shows the inverse relationship between deductible and premium.

Figure 7-1

Annual Deductible	Annual Premium
$100	$2,819
$250	$2,630
$500	$2,514
$1,000	$2,467

You probably should not report a small claim because it will affect your future insurance rates. This is true even if the claim wasn't your fault. You have to ask yourself if a $200 claim is worth reporting and getting reimbursed if the insurance company turns around and raises your rates the next year.

As a result, why would you want to pay for a $100 or $250 deductible if you don't plan to file a claim for this small amount? In our example in Figure 7-1, this leaves the $500 and $1,000 deductible. The question to ask yourself is if an additional $47 in annual premium is worth having a deductible that's $500 lower. Based on the numbers, I recommend the $500 deductible with this actual example, but you may want to roll the dice that you won't get into an accident this year. While Figure 7-1 is an auto policy example, the same concept is true for a homeowners policy.

Considering deductibles when purchasing auto and home insurance will give you comfort and peace of mind knowing you have the appropriate protection for the least amount of money. This is especially true when something happens like an automobile accident or a fire in your home and you're forced to pay the deductible.

Don't make the mistake of not knowing what your deductible is until you actually have to file a claim. You may end up being surprised that your deductible is really high, and you may be hard-pressed to pay this amount. Be an active consumer and consider deductibles when you're purchasing your auto and home insurance.

How Do I Take Action?

When you shop around for your insurance, ask the agents for quotes/prices based on different deductible amounts. Analyze these numbers to choose the best premium and deductible for your unique circumstances.

Remember to be realistic. Don't choose the lowest premium if it would be a hardship to pay the deductible if something actually happened. Accidents happen even if you don't think you'll ever be in one. You're better off being prepared for when and not if you're in an accident. I personally have been hit by other drivers on numerous occasions. You can't predict when you'll be in an accident.

Don't be passive and take whatever the insurance agent quotes you. You should ask for the premiums based on different deductibles, and you should do this for both your auto and homeowners insurance policies.

Taking the time to bring this to a conscious level by asking your insurance agent for quotes on premiums and deductibles will provide you with the best coverage at the best price for your current situation/circumstances. As circumstances change, you may also want to change your deductibles. Doing this will prevent you from being shocked when something happens. Implementing this action item will bring you peace of mind knowing you made an educated conscious decision that you won't regret should something happen with your auto or home.

Action 30

I will keep my auto insurance rates down.

Why Should I Take Action?

Auto insurance premiums vary greatly from company to company and even within the same company. Premiums are based on numerous variables. Some of these variables are out of our control. For example, you will pay more for your auto insurance if you're 16 versus being 21. Similarly, a 21-year-old will pay more than a 26-year-old. Typically, people under 25 are considered a higher risk. Males will also typically pay more than females because they're also considered a higher risk.

However, some things are in our control as it relates to getting and maintaining the lowest auto insurance rates possible. Claim history and good credit are two of the most important variables in keeping your auto insurance rates down.

Every company has its own framework or models to determine how much it will raise your rate for submitting a claim, as well as how much it will charge you based on your credit score.

At-fault accident claims are often worse because insurers now assess you as a higher-risk driver, and higher risk translates to higher premiums.

According to WalletHub[18], the average car insurance premium will go up by 50% the following year after an at-fault accident. The exact amount will ultimately depend on a few factors, including your insurance company, the state you live in, and the extent of the damage.

Another factor to keep in mind is the possibility of having another claim shortly after your first. The insurance company will either raise your premium significantly again or drop you altogether. Imagine the insurance company dropping you and having to find another insurance company that would want to take the risk of providing you auto insurance after you just filed your second claim. Good luck!

Another variable in your control is traffic tickets (speeding, not coming to a complete stop, etc.). NerdWallet found car insurance usually goes up by 25% after a traffic ticket.[19] This obviously depends on your insurance company along with many other factors such as age, gender, and the state you live in.

One of the things my dad used to say is "It doesn't pay to speed," and this is definitely true when it comes to the extra insurance premium you may have to pay after getting a traffic ticket.

Most insurance companies look back at your driving record for the past three to five years. This means you may be paying higher auto insurance rates for the next three to five years.

One way to keep traffic tickets off your record is to take a supervision class when offered by the court system. While the specifics are different from state to state, my state requires a one-time four-hour defensive driving class that keeps the traffic ticket off your record. To me, it's worth the four hours to avoid your auto premium going up 25% or more.

Good credit, driving safely to avoid accidents, and traffic tickets are all variables in our control. All of these help us keep our auto insurance rates lower, stretch our earnings, and help us achieve our goals faster.

How Do I Take Action?

We've learned throughout this book that credit score plays a substantial role in how much we pay for a variety of things. One of these is how much you'll pay for auto insurance. To that end, establish and maintain a good credit score to keep your auto rates lower. This is easier said than done for some people. The most important thing to remember to make this happen is to not spend more money than you can afford. This will allow you to pay your entire credit card bill on time every month, which helps your credit score.

The second important variable in how much you pay in auto insurance is claim history. This means you need to drive safely and stay out of accidents. This can be more challenging, as accidents sometimes just happen. But as explained before, part of this is not turning in small claims to your insurance company because they'll raise your rates. In the end, the small claim isn't worth the extra money you'll pay in premiums.

Some other variables that affect your auto insurance rates, which you can utilize for many insurance companies, include:

- Reducing coverage on older cars.
- Taking advantage of low-mileage discounts.
- Comparing insurance costs before you buy a car.
- Increasing your deductible.
- Checking to see what discounts you qualify for.
- Comparing auto insurance quotes.
- Maintaining a good driving record.
- Participating in a safe driving program.
- Taking a defensive driving course.
- Exploring payment options.

Doing these things can help you save money on your auto insurance premiums, stretch your earnings, and help you achieve your goals faster.

Action **31**

I will carry more than the state-required
coverage limits on my auto insurance.

Background Knowledge

Coverage Limits – The maximum amount your insurance company will pay on a claim. You are responsible for any amount above the coverage limit. Insurance companies will list coverage limits using three numbers. For example, 25/50/20 coverage limits represent the following per accident:

- $25,000 (bodily injury single) maximum amount paid per person for bodily injury.

- $50,000 (bodily injury, total) maximum amount paid for bodily injuries to two or more people.

- $20,000 (property damage) maximum amount paid for property damage.

Insurance companies all have coverage limits, which reduce their overall liability.

Why Should I Take Action?

The minimum coverage amount you must have by law varies by state. However, the minimum coverage required by law in each state is not adequate if you get into an automobile accident. What does this mean?

If you don't have adequate coverage limits and you're in a car accident that is your fault, you will have to pay the amount beyond your coverage limits. For example, in Illinois, the coverage limits are 25/50/20. If you cause an accident and the medical bills and property damage caused by the accident are more than $25,000/$50,000/$20,000, then you must pay for everything above these amounts. This expense will come out of your pocket. This could be a significant amount of money and could cause financial hardship that may stay with you for the rest of your life.

Is this really worth it? Absolutely NOT!

You also may be affected even if you aren't at fault. People often forget that auto insurance will pay for your medical bills and property damage if you're hit by an uninsured or underinsured driver.

Unfortunately, I have a sad story to share from my friend who is an insurance agent. A client of his was on a motorcycle when he was hit and killed by an uninsured drunk driver. However, because his client had insurance, the policy paid his wife $250,000—the amount of the coverage limit.

The difference in premium for higher coverage limits is minor compared to the risks you incur by burying your head in the sand and hoping nothing ever happens.

For example, the difference between 100/300/100 and 500/500/100 on my two vehicles is $80 per year. It's well worth the $80 to know we will be adequately covered if someone in my family is the cause of a horrific accident, or if we're hit by an uninsured motorist.

Having appropriate coverage limits will also prevent the potential financial hardship caused by insufficient coverage limits. Don't risk the small amount of extra money on your premium to get appropriate coverage, as it's not worth the risk.

Have peace of mind that you won't cause you and your family financial hardship should you be the cause of a tragic accident.

How Do I Take Action?

How much coverage do you need? I currently have 250,000/500,000/250,000 and you may want even more coverage. Ask your insurance agent for quotes on the different coverage limits, analyze the numbers, and decide on coverage limits that won't cause financial hardship down the road.

This is not something to roll the dice with. This also should give you comfort and peace of mind knowing you have the protection you need if you're at fault and cause a multi-car accident that results in expensive medical bills, property damage, or death.

Action 32

I will determine if I need rental car insurance.

Background Knowledge

Loss-of-Use Coverage – This coverage pays you if get into an accident while driving a rental car and the rental company can't rent the car to someone else while the car is being repaired. There may be a clause in the rental car agreement saying you owe so much per day to cover their inability to rent the car to someone else. Loss-of-use coverage will also pay in this scenario. However, this is a special endorsement, and not all insurance companies offer it.

Diminished-Value Coverage – Coverage if you're in an accident while driving a rental car and the car rental company says it won't make as much when it sells the vehicle because of the damage. Diminished-Value Coverage is a special endorsement, and not all insurance companies offer it.

Why Should I Take Action?

Let's say you're taking a trip and need to rent a car so you can explore your destination. When you go to rent the car, they'll ask you if you want rental car insurance. They may charge you an additional $50 per day for this coverage. If you're renting the car for a week, this could be an additional $350 for a week-long vacation. Why would you purchase rental car insurance if you already have coverage through your automobile insurance or through your credit card (some credit cards offer rental car coverage)?

If you're like most people and have liability and property damage on your auto policy, then you're usually covered for those same things on a rental car. Don't waste your money on this if you already have coverage. Think about how much money this could add up to if you take one or more vacations per year; year after year of paying for this when you absolutely don't need the duplicate coverage. Declining this coverage when you already have coverage will save you money, stretch your earnings, and help you achieve your goals faster.

How Do I Take Action?

Read the rental car agreement carefully. Some rental agreements have two clauses to look out for. These include loss-of-use coverage and diminished-value coverage. If these clauses are in the rental agreement, make sure you have these endorsements on your automobile insurance policy. This is worth exploring even if you only rent a car once a year. The money adds up, and why waste it when you don't need to? You can look at your automobile insurance coverage directly or call your insurance agent to inquire about it.

If you don't currently have these coverages on your auto insurance policy, you may want to add loss-of-use coverage and diminished-value coverage, as this may save you money in the long run.

Also, look at your credit card agreement; some credit cards offer rental car insurance. You'll need to use the credit card to pay for the rental car for the insurance to be valid.

As stated before, if you fail to plan, you plan to fail. Do a little research in advance of your vacations so that you can save money if you rent a car. This is time well spent, as it can save you thousands of dollars over your lifetime for duplicate coverage you don't need.

Action 33

I will consider purchasing renters' insurance.

Why Should I Take Action?

You should consider purchasing renters' insurance because it's inexpensive and a means of protection from financial loss. Insurance companies will ask you to pick a content coverage number of how much you want or need. For example, if you say you want $20,000 content coverage, the premium is around $150 per year. The price will depend on the state and city you live in. If there is a fire, or if someone breaks into your apartment or rental house and steals your belongings, insurance will pay for your contents up to $20,000.

Renters' insurance also comes with liability insurance, medical insurance, and loss of use. Liability insurance provides coverage if someone gets hurt on your property because you were at fault.

In this case, liability insurance pays the medical bills of the injured person. It also pays your court costs if someone gets hurt on your property and sues you. The medical portion pays for someone who gets hurt on your property and you were found to be not liable or at fault. Loss of use pays for you to live elsewhere temporarily. For example, if there's a fire and you need to live somewhere while your place is being fixed, loss of use will cover your lodgings.

You may not want to purchase renters' insurance. However, I want you to be aware of how cheap it is for the amount of coverage that you get.

One of my nephews purchased renters' insurance when he was in college mainly because his rental home was not in the best neighborhood. As fate would have it, his rental home was burglarized and his laptop was stolen, among other things. The rental insurance paid for him to get a new laptop. This obviously was a lot more money than the little rental insurance premium and was obviously the right decision for him.

How Do I Take Action?

Ask your insurance agent for a renters' insurance quote. Doing this won't cost you anything, and having the actual number will help you make an informed decision. If you don't have an insurance agent, be sure to read Action 27 before moving forward. Having the knowledge of how much the renters' insurance will cost is part of being a well-informed consumer.

Action 34

I will purchase floater policy insurance.

Background Knowledge

Floater Policy – Purchased on your homeowner's insurance policy, this covers expensive items that are movable, such as jewelry.

Why Should I Take Action?

The most common item to purchase floater policy insurance on is an engagement ring. According to American Express, a one-carat engagement ring typically costs around $5,500, but most couples spend over $6,000 and 7% of people spend over $10,000.[20]

You have to hear the true story about one of my cousins. He went out for dinner with his wife. After dinner, his wife went to the restroom, where she took her wedding ring off to wash her hands.

They had driven all the way home before she realized her wedding ring was missing. By the time they'd driven back to the restaurant and looked in the bathroom, the wedding ring was gone.

The ring was worth over $10,000 at the time. Because they had the ring insured on a floater policy, the insurance company sent them a check for the value of the ring.

Another example of something that happens from time to time is the actual diamond falling out of a ring's setting. Many factors go into this, like the type of setting, the age of the setting, and more.

In general, a floater policy on your wedding ring costs about $10 per $1,000. For example, insuring a wedding ring with a value of $10,000 will cost you $100 per year. This is worth the money to make sure your valuable belongings are covered if something happens.

How Do I Take Action?

This is really quite simple. Just ask your insurance agent for a quote for insuring something on a floater policy. The most common item is a wedding ring. The insurance agent will ask you to have the item appraised so they know how much to insure it for. The insured item will appear on your homeowner's policy and will be listed separately, along with the price to insure.

Action 35

I will consider purchasing umbrella coverage.

Background Knowledge

Umbrella Coverage – Extra liability coverage that provides insurance protection beyond coverages on other policies like auto and home insurance. Figure 7-2 provides a good illustration of how umbrella coverage offers protection above and beyond your home, auto, and personal coverage.

Figure 7-2[21]

Why Should I Take Action?

There is a direct correlation between how much you have in assets and how much you need in an umbrella policy. The more you have to lose, the more umbrella insurance you should consider.

For example, let's look at a true story from a good friend who has been an insurance agent for over 25 years. He had a client who we'll call Will B. Dunn. Will had an adverse reaction to a medication and passed out while driving. He crossed traffic and hit two other vehicles. One of the parties was severely injured and sued Will for more than $1 million.

This story ends well because fortunately, Will had an umbrella policy. If he hadn't had an umbrella policy, his personal assets would have been threatened, putting him in a tough financial situation.

This would have been a large financial hole that would have affected the rest of his life. Would he ever be able to retire with financial freedom? Would he be forced to work into his 70s?

To protect yourself from a similar situation, consider purchasing an umbrella policy. For example, for an additional $200 to $250 premium per year, you can be covered for an additional $1 million. This protection will pay for medical bills, property damage, and lawsuits.

Some umbrella policies include coverage for:
- A serious automobile accident where you are the cause of the accident.
- Someone falls and is injured in your yard or in your home.
- Your dog bites someone.
- A neighbor falls in your pool and drowns.
- One of your son's friends falls off the trampoline and breaks a leg.

In Action 31, we learned about coverage limits. In Figure 7-3, we look at coverage limits and how they play a role in umbrella coverage.

Figure 7-3

Type of Insurance	Limits of Liability
Automobile Bodily Injury Property Damage	**Per Accident** $300,000 $100,000
Home Liability Medical	**Per Accident** $300,000 $2,000

Figure 7-3 provides an example of coverage limits for auto and home insurance policies. Say you're in an automobile accident in which you were at fault and caused $500,000 worth of bodily injury (medical bills) and $200,000 worth of property damage.

In this simple yet realistic example, your auto policy would pay $300,000 for bodily injury and $100,000 for property damage, meaning you'd still be on the hook for the additional $300,000 in expenses. However, nothing would come out of your pocket if you had an umbrella policy equal to or greater than the additional expenses.

The same would be true if someone had an accident and broke their leg on a trampoline at your home. Your homeowners insurance would pay a maximum of $300,000 if you were sued, and $2,000 for medical injuries.

Because the umbrella policy provides coverage over your auto as well as your homeowner's insurance, you would be covered. The umbrella policy would pay the additional money if a child fell off a trampoline and broke their leg at your house, and their parents sued you for pain and suffering.

Unfortunately, you're more likely to be sued when you have a lot to lose. An umbrella policy is not a lot of money for this additional protection. Think about what happened to Will, which truly could happen to anyone. Fortunately for him, he purchased an umbrella policy to pay for the lawsuit. What about you?

How Do I Take Action?

If you read this book and implement the action statements, one day you will have a lot to lose because you chose to TAKE ACTION and have significant assets. I'm proud of you for implementing these action statements. This action statement is easy because all you need to do is call your insurance agent and ask them to give you a quote for umbrella coverage. The most common amount is $1 million, but you could ask for more if needed. This should bring you comfort and peace of mind knowing you have extra protection over your existing auto and home policies.

Action 36

I will determine my best healthcare option each year.

Background Knowledge

Your employer will share their healthcare options on an annual basis and give you time to decide what coverage you want for the upcoming year. At this time, you'll need to choose a healthcare insurance option.

Employer-Sponsored Health Coverage – Health insurance obtained through your employer.

Open Enrollment Period – Time given once a year to enroll in your employer's health insurance plan and other benefits for the next calendar year.

Health Maintenance Organization (HMO) – A type of health insurance plan that typically limits coverage of care to doctors within the network. Insurance won't pay for out-of-network care except in an emergency. In exchange for this limitation, it can be less expensive.

Preferred Provider Organization (PPO) – A type of plan where you pay less to see in-network doctors. Insurance pays (a smaller percentage) if you choose to go to doctors and hospitals outside of the network (see co-insurance).

Primary Care Provider – A healthcare professional who practices general medicine. With an HMO, this is your first stop for care.

Co-Insurance – The percentage of costs split between you and the insurer after your deductible is met. For example, in an 80/20 co-insurance plan, the insurance company pays 80% and you pay 20% until you reach a certain limit. Your plan will have a maximum co-insurance dollar amount you must pay per calendar year. Co-insurance percentages typically have you pay more of the percentage when you go outside the network. For example, co-insurance may be 80/20 for in-network and 60/40 for out-of-network. In this example, you pay 40% for going outside of your network instead of 20% for staying in your network.

Co-Payments – The amount you're required to pay for each doctor visit or medicine purchase. Typical co-payments are $25 or less.

Figure 7-4 lists the pros and cons of HMO and PPO options.

Figure 7-4

Pros of an HMO	Pros of a PPO
• Typically lower premiums • Low or no deductibles	• No referral needed to see a specialist. • Usually has some out-of-network coverage.
Cons of an HMO	Cons of a PPO
• Must see in-network doctors. • Usually need a referral from your Primary Care Physician to see a specialist.	• Higher premiums • Higher deductibles

Why Should I Take Action?

Each year, your employer will have an open enrollment period for your health insurance options. This is important to analyze each year for many reasons, including competing variables between coverage and cost. The first variable to consider is coverage. You want to make sure you and your family are adequately covered.

Many employers offer at least one PPO and one HMO option. The HMO option will be far less expensive throughout the year. You may ask, then, why doesn't everyone go with the HMO option? The answer is coverage.

Let me share a story to illustrate my point. Fortunately, my parents and grandparents didn't suffer from heart conditions or cancer, and they all lived well into their late 80s and 90s. I inherited these wonderful genes and am rarely sick. In 33 years, there was only one instance where I was too sick to go to work. I haven't had a need to go to the doctor very often. As a result of being blessed with good health, when I started my first job out of college, I chose an HMO option from my employer. Why? The HMO saved me a whole lot of money. I chose the HMO option year after year, which saved me thousands of dollars. I did this until I was married.

After being blessed with my wonderful wife, we then chose one of the PPO options. Why would I do this knowing I'd have to pay more? My wife is not blessed with healthy genes and has several autoimmune diseases. As a result, she has a need to see specialists in different health-related fields.

While the HMO is cheaper, it won't pay for doctors who are not in the network. This would restrict and force my wife to go to doctors on a list and not doctors who came strongly recommended.

Paying significantly more for a PPO option has been worth the money to us to have better coverage. What I mean by coverage is the freedom to choose the doctors that she believes can help her the most. In exchange for this freedom, we had more money taken out of my paycheck for the PPO as well as more out-of-pocket money spent on deductibles and co-insurance.

Take a close look at your health and your family's overall health. Look at the various options given to you by your employer and make an informed decision. This decision has an impact on medical coverage as well as how much money is taken out of your check to pay for the health insurance, and out-of-pocket money spent on deductibles, co-insurance, and co-payments.

Typically, this is a decision you'll have to live with for one calendar year until the next open enrollment period, so it's important to get it right based on your circumstances. Taking the time to analyze and choose the best option for you and your family will bring peace of mind and hopefully no regrets throughout the year.

How Do I Take Action?

Your employer will send out their benefits package each year and give you time to decide which coverage you want for the year. This is called the open enrollment period. During the open enrollment period, your employer shares how much each healthcare option will cost per paycheck as well as the specifics of each health insurance option. Here is an example so that you'll have a better understanding of how it works.

Figure 7-5 shows a typical example of three insurance choices and how much money would be taken out of your biweekly paycheck. Every employer will be different in the choices they offer and how much money comes out of your check. As Figure 7-5 illustrates, it's very common to charge different rates for just you, you and your spouse, or you and your family. This makes perfect sense as the more people use the insurance, the more expensive it will be for your employer, who usually passes the added expense on to you.

Figure 7-5

Insurance Plan	Just You	You and Spouse	Family
HMO	$9	$22	$34
PPO	$79	$152	$270
High Deductible PPO	$43	$84	$146

Figure 7-5 also shows the major differences in money taken out of your biweekly paycheck. In this realistic example, the difference in money taken out of your paycheck between an HMO and a PPO for a family per year is $6,136. I share this amount with you to emphasize the importance of analyzing your choices.

Figure 7-6 (opposite page)
This figure illustrates a simplified version of what else your employer typically gives you each year during the open enrollment period. This gives specific details on each option offered to you so you can make a more informed decision.

Analyze the numbers carefully to determine the best plan for your health needs and budget. Look at your health history. Ask if either of your parents has a heart condition, diabetes, cancer, or any other life-impacting issues. There's no one-size-fits-all when it comes to health benefits.

Plan Provision	HMO	PPO		High Deductible PPO	
	In-network only	In-network	Out-of-network	In-network	Out-of-network
Calendar year medical deductible (individual/family)	$200/ $600	$500/ $1,500	$800/ $2,400	$2,800/ $5,600	
Coinsurance	Plan pays 100% after deductible	Plan pays 90% after deductible	Plan pays 70% after deductible	Plan pays 90% after deductible	Plan pays 70% after deductible
Medical out-of-pocket maximums (deductibles, copayments, coinsurance apply)	$2,600/ $5,200	$3,100/ $6,200	$6,200/ $12,400	$3,800/ $7,600	$5,800/ $11,600
Office visits	$25 copay then pays 100%	$25 copay then pays 100%	Pays 70% after deductible	Pays 90% after deductible	Pays 70% after deductible
Outpatient surgery	$100 copay then pays 100%	$100 copay then 90% after deductible	Pays 70% after deductible	Pays 90% after deductible	Pays 70% after deductible
Emergency room services	$250 copay then pays 100%	$250 copay then pays 100%	$250 copay then pays 100%	Pays 90% after deductible	Pays 90% after deductible

As I mentioned earlier, the selections you make usually stay in effect for one calendar year. However, some companies may let you change your selection if you have something called "qualifying life events" such as getting married or the birth of a child.

Taking some time to analyze all of the information can help you make an informed decision on the competing variables between coverage and cost. Analyzing your options should give you some peace of mind knowing you chose the best option for you and your family for the upcoming year.

It should be noted that if you're not offered health insurance from your employer, you'll need to get an individual plan through the Affordable Care Act. You can go to healthcare.gov and apply online or call them and apply over the phone. It's wise to get help from an insurance agent, but bear in mind that not all agents handle health insurance.

Action 37

I will take advantage of my employer's
flexible spending account (FSA) or
health savings account (HSA).

Background Knowledge

Flexible Spending Account (FSA) – An account you put money into to pay for out-of-pocket health care costs. You don't pay any income taxes on this money. Because of the tax benefits, the IRS limits the amount you can put into a FSA. The drawback to an FSA is you will lose any money you don't use during the year.

Health Savings Account (HSA) – Similar to an FSA where you put money into an account to pay for out-of-pocket health care costs and you don't pay any income taxes on this money. The IRS also limits the amount you can put into a HSA. The major differences are that you have to be enrolled in an HSA-eligible healthcare plan, and you don't have to spend the money in one calendar year. In other words, the money carries over from year to year. An HSA may also be funded by contributions from your employer, from you, or both.

Why Should I Take Action?

Your employer is not required to offer either option, but many offer an HSA or an FSA. As stated earlier, you have to be enrolled in an HSA-eligible healthcare plan to contribute to an HSA. If your employer offers an HSA, I strongly recommend using it because of the money you can save in taxes, which we'll illustrate in this action statement.

We're going to move ahead in learning about FSAs in this action statement to illustrate the importance of figuring out how much you'll spend on healthcare costs in a calendar year. This is critical information to know, as you'll lose the money at the end of the calendar year if you don't use it. An FSA is a use-it-or-lose-it proposition.

Let me use a story about my son needing braces to illustrate why you should take action on your employer's FSA. My son's dentist let us know that he would eventually need braces. The dentist sent us to an orthodontist, who agreed my son would eventually need braces. However, he told us it would be best to wait a year or two until his baby teeth came out.

The open enrollment for our insurance occurs every November. During this open enrollment period, we estimate how much money to put into our FSA. When I asked my wife about braces for my son, she said the dentist felt it was still a year away.

A few months later, the surprise happened. When we went for a checkup, the orthodontist felt it was time to have braces put on. This was very different from what he said before. Why was this a disappointment from a financial point of view?

The cost of braces was $5,000. At that time, we were in the 24% tax bracket. How much did this surprise "he's now ready for braces" cost in taxes? We could have saved $1,200 in income taxes had we not been surprised by the orthodontist. That's a lot of money we could have used elsewhere.

Let's look at a second example in chart form to help you visualize the tax savings. In Figure 7-7, we look at someone who is single, makes $60,000, and estimates they'll have $2,000 in out-of-pocket medical expenses for the year.

Figure 7-7

	No FSA	With FSA
Adjusted Gross Income	$60,000	$60,000
Subtract FSA Contributions	-0-	$2,000
= Taxable Income	$60,000	$58,000
22% Tax Bracket	$13,200	$12,760
= Tax Savings	-0-	$440

As you can see from the two examples, taking the time to estimate your health-related costs for the year is well worth the time. Doing this every year will add up to a significant amount of money saved in income taxes throughout your life. This is especially true considering the amount you put into an FSA will be much higher when you have a family. Doing this every year will save you money in taxes, which ultimately stretches your earnings and helps you achieve your goals faster.

How Do I Take Action?

Most people have predictable ongoing medical expenses throughout the year, and using pre-tax dollars lowers your overall cost. How can you take action on these expenses? My wife and I keep a simple spreadsheet throughout the year that we use to track our out-of-pocket medical expenses. The spreadsheet contains the date, the person in our family being treated, a brief description of the issue, and the amount. The description can be very brief, like "chiropractic adjustment" or "broken arm."

As stated earlier, our open enrollment through our employers occurs in November. We look at our FSA spreadsheet to decide how much we should put into our FSA for the following year.

Having this information from the spreadsheet makes it easy for us to maximize this tax benefit. If you have a family, you'll probably be shocked at how much you actually spend out of pocket on health-related expenses. We also have an annual conversation if we think there will be any changes either up or down in our out-of-pocket medical expenses.

Money is taken out of each paycheck pre-tax and put into our FSA account. We get a debit card for our FSA and use it for the appropriate expenses. Examples of appropriate expenses include health plan co-payments and deductibles, dental work including orthodontics, prescription drugs, eyeglasses, contact lenses, and medical devices. The IRS limits your contributions to an FSA; in 2023, that limit was $3,050.

We keep all of our receipts when we use the FSA debit card, and once in a while, the company managing the FSA will ask to see a receipt electronically. This little bit of extra work is worth the money saved. Why would we want to pay more money in income taxes when we don't have to?

Chapter 8

Becoming a Parent: Now What?

What becomes of my family if something happens to me? How will I pay for my children's college? Learn three important actions to take when you have a family.

You're over-the-moon excited because you're expecting your first child. I didn't sleep for weeks when my wife and I found out we were expecting. My mind raced with anticipation as I lay in bed wide awake, thinking of all of the things I wanted to do with my son. I envisioned playing sports, traveling, and fishing. I thought about teaching him how to ride a bike, drive a car, and most importantly, what it meant to be a caring, compassionate, loving person.

There was also the reality that set in that my wife and I were now responsible for another human being. We quickly learned there were three important and almost vital steps we had to quickly take care of to have peace of mind when our son was born. In the next three action statements, I will go into depth on these steps.

Action 38

I will purchase term life insurance.

Background Knowledge

Note: This action statement also fits under our insurance chapter. However, I wanted to keep together the three important steps when becoming a parent.

Life Insurance – Insurance that pays a sum of money to your beneficiary upon your death.

Beneficiary – The person or persons that you designate to receive the money from your life insurance policy in the event of your death.

Group Life Insurance – Life insurance offered through your work as part of your benefits package. This type of insurance ceases when you change jobs or retire.

Individual Life Insurance – Life insurance you purchase on your own.

Term Life Insurance – Inexpensive life insurance coverage for a specified period (usually 10 or 20 years) where in exchange for paying an annual premium, the insurance company agrees to pay a specified amount to your beneficiaries upon your death.

Permanent Life Insurance – As the name implies, permanent life insurance offers coverage for the duration of your life. In exchange for paying an annual premium, the insurer agrees to pay a specified amount upon your death. This type of policy also offers a cash value.

Cash Value – With a permanent life insurance policy, a portion of your premium goes toward insuring your life, while the other portion goes toward building up a cash value. The cash value can grow at a fixed or variable interest rate, and it grows tax deferred. You also may be able to borrow against the cash value portion of your policy.

Why Should I Take Action?

When you get married and have a family, you should purchase life insurance. Take a minute to think about the financial hardship if you unexpectedly pass away and your family can no longer count on your paycheck. That's not a very good image, but it's a reality check. The financial hardship would be above and beyond the emotional hardship left for your family. During these difficult times, do you want your family to be taken care of or struggle financially?

Life insurance will help protect your spouse and children from the financial hardship that could result if something happened to you. The money can be used to help cover essential expenses like paying off your mortgage, day care, sending your children to college, paying off your debt, paying for your funeral, and even replacing some of your income.

There are two broad types of life insurance policies: term and permanent life insurance. Within the permanent life insurance policies there are several different options, which we won't get into because I strongly recommend purchasing term life insurance. Why? Term insurance is pure insurance with no sales gimmicks and gives you the coverage you need at an affordable price.

In Figure 8-1, we price $500,000 term life insurance for a 30-year-old non-smoking male. In the "How Long" column, we see 10-, 15-, 20-, and 30-year terms. This number represents how long the insurance coverage at this premium amount will last.

Figure 8-1

How Long	Amount	Annual Premium
10-Year Term	$500,000	$215
15-Year Term	$500,000	$230
20-Year Term	$500,000	$250
30-Year Term	$500,000	$335

In Figure 8-2, we price $500,000 term life insurance for a 30-year-old non-smoking female.

Figure 8-2

How Long	Amount	Annual Premium
10-Year Term	$500,000	$195
15-Year Term	$500,000	$200
20-Year Term	$500,000	$210
30-Year Term	$500,000	$285

We learn in Figures 8-1 and 8-2 that females' annual premiums are less than males for the same insurance. The reason for this is that statistically, women live longer than men and therefore are considered less at risk of dying, so they pay a smaller annual premium for the same insurance.

In Figure 8-3, we price $500,000 permanent life insurance for a 30-year-old female and a 30-year-old male.

Figure 8-3

How Long	Amount	Annual Premium
Whole Life	$500,000	$2,526 female
Whole life	$500,000	$2,767 male

Why am I recommending term insurance? In Figures 8-1, 8-2, and 8-3, we learn that a 20-year term has an annual premium of $250 for a 30-year-old male and $210 for a 30-year-old female, and permanent insurance costs $2,767 for a 30-year-old male and $2,526 for a 30-year-old female.

Wow! That's a significant difference, and this difference is paid every single year.

Some insurance agents will push the permanent life insurance policy because they make a much higher commission compared to term insurance.

I had this happen to me before my brother became an insurance agent. The salesperson made it look and sound so good. This was from someone I went to middle school with who called me before I was married and had children. This was also before I knew much about life insurance. After analyzing the numbers, I chose not to purchase the insurance.

I thought, *Why do I need life insurance with no dependents?*

Don't buy something you don't need yet.

With permanent insurance, a portion of your premium goes toward building up a cash value. The cash value can grow at a fixed or variable interest rate, and it grows tax deferred.

However, the actual return on your investment is typically not very high.

Instead, you can purchase a term life insurance policy and invest the money you would have spent on a permanent life policy with the freedom to choose where you want to invest your money, and you can typically get a much higher return on your investment.

Figure 8-4 gives us a visual representation of the major difference in annual premiums between term and permanent insurance.

Figure 8-4

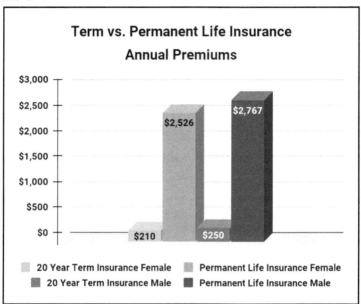

Remember, these are annual premiums, so think about the significantly higher premium you're spending year after year over a 20-year period.

In Figure 8-5, we look at the term and permanent life insurance cost of a $500,000 insurance policy over 20 years for both a female and a male.

Ask yourself: *Why do I need life insurance?* To take care of your loved ones when you're gone. Term life insurance does this really well at a fraction of the cost. Term pays salespeople far less in commissions, so they may push permanent insurance on you. Now you know better. Buy term insurance and invest the rest.

Don't waste your money on sales commissions and on insurance you don't need after your children are grown up and no longer dependent on you.

Figure 8-5

Type of Insurance	Annual Premium	Cost Over 20 Years
20-Year Term Female	$210	$4,200
20-Year Term Male	$250	$5,000
Permanent Female	$2,526	$50,520
Permanent Male	$2,767	$55,340

How Do I Take Action?

The first thing you need to determine is how much life insurance you need for your loved ones. This is not easy. You can Google "how much life insurance do I need calculator" and you'll find numerous choices. This can be used to help you determine the appropriate amount.

To get an accurate assessment, add up the financial obligations you want covered and then subtract the assets you own that could be used, such as investments, savings, and group life insurance policies through your employer.

Some things to consider include your annual income, marital status, age, debt, number of children, day care, cost of college, funeral expenses, and income replacement. Your insurance agent can also help you determine how much life insurance you need.

Once you figure out the amount you need, you can shop around

(Action 27) for term life insurance. The most popular is a 20-year level term policy. The advantage of the 20-year level term policy over the 10-year level term policy is the consistently lower price.

If you take out a 10-year level term policy when you have your first child, they'll only be 10 years old when the policy is finished. Most families still need life insurance when their first child is still only 10 years old, so when you go to purchase another 10-year term policy, you are now 10 years older and the premium price will be higher.

If you take out a 20-year level term policy when you have your first child, the policy will last for the next 20 years, as will the premium. This way, you avoid the more expensive premium you would have to pay if you first purchased the 10-year term policy. Why? Because the older you get, the more expensive your premium will be.

As your circumstances change, you may find you need to take out another term life insurance policy. For example, if you have a second or third child. Another option is to consider a 30-year level term policy if you plan on having multiple children.

My wife and I have a life insurance policy on me. If something were to happen to me, my wife and son would be financially protected. However, we chose not to take out a life insurance policy on my wife other than the group life insurance policy offered through her employer as one of her benefits.

Being the major breadwinner in the family, we decided I would be financially okay if something happened to her. This has nothing to do with the emotional side of losing her.

All circumstances are different, but 20-year or 30-year level term policies make sense for most families. Talk this over with your spouse and decide which option is best for your family.

To summarize, buy term insurance at a fraction of the cost and stay away from permanent insurance. Doing this will give you the protection you need for your family, save you significant money, stretch your earnings, and help you achieve your goals in life.

Action 39

I will take advantage of 529 college
savings plans for my children.

Background Knowledge

529 College Savings Plan – Works similarly to a Roth IRA where
you contribute after-tax dollars but your investment grows tax-free
when used to pay for tuition, books, and other college expenses.
As we learned in Action 2 about Roth IRAs, a significant amount
of money is saved when you don't have to pay federal income taxes
on the interest you earn over the years.

Besides the federal income tax advantages, there also may be
state income tax advantages. For example, in Illinois, contributions
made to a 529 college savings plan can be deducted up to $10,000
per year for an individual and $20,000 per year for a married cou-
ple. There are two types of 529 plans, including education savings
plans and prepaid tuition plans.

Why Should I Take Action?

When we were expecting our first child, I thought about the
financial side of raising a child. In just 19 short years, my
son would be going to college. This turned out to be very quick
years, as my son is now in high school. Trust me when I say it will
be here before you know it.

You can look forward to four years of tuition, housing, food,
transportation, books, and other school-related fees. Unfortunately, tuition and fees have significantly outpaced inflation over
the last 20 years, and there is no reason to believe they won't continue to outpace inflation.

Chapter 8: Becoming a Parent: Now What?

Let's take a look at some alarming data. According to Melanie Hanson of Educationdata.org[22]

- The average cost of college in the United States is $35,551 per student per year.
- The annual cost of college has more than doubled in the 21st century, with an annual growth rate of 7.1%.
- The average private non-profit university student spends $54,501 per year.
- Student borrowers pay an average of $2,186 in interest each year, and the average student borrower spends roughly 20 years paying off their school loans.
- From 2000 to 2020, average college tuition inflation outpaced wage inflation by 111.4%.

These statistics don't exactly make us feel good about paying for college. This is actually kind of scary. We know college will be expensive, and with multiple children, it'll be very expensive. What can we do about it?

One option is to do what many people do, which is to bury your head in the sand and save very little for your children's college education. When it's time to pay for your children's education, you end up taking out massive loans to pay for college. Some people who do this delay their retirement significantly because they have such large student loan debts. I hope you've learned enough from reading this book to know this isn't a good option. Putting your head in the sand and doing nothing usually is not a good option for anything and only hamstrings your future.

Another option is to have your children pay for all or some of their college education. This option typically leads to massive loans for your child and will saddle them with debt after graduation. Think about how much college tuition will be when your newborn goes off to college. Ouch!!! I also want to reiterate that it takes the average student borrower 20 years to pay off their school loans.

My wife and I made the conscious decision that we wanted to pay for our son's college education so he wasn't saddled with debt after graduation. I recognize this is also easier for us as we were unfortunately able to have only one child. I also recognize every situation is different and you may want your child to have "some skin in the game."

With the average cost of college across the United States being $35,551 per year, most people wouldn't be able to pay for this by writing a check without having saved a whole lot of money well in advance. As we learned about compound interest with our 401(k), the time to start investing for college is when your child is born. Like retirement, the earlier the better. I started the same year my son was born, so I practiced what I preach.

With that said, why should we use a 529 college savings plan? Why can't I put some money aside or invest some money on my own? As we learned earlier about 401(k) tax advantages (Action 2), there are significant tax advantages with a 529 college savings plan.

There are two types of 529 plans: education savings plans and prepaid tuition plans. You should take action on one of these. Let's first look at education savings plans.

Education Savings Plans
Similar to the rationale and argument we learned in Action 2 where we're using a Roth IRA, we should also take advantage of a 529 college savings plan.

The tax advantages are significant. How much would you save in taxes? Let's look at an example where you contribute $250 per month in a 529 college savings plan for 22 years until your new-born graduates from college. Using the same 10.12% interest we used with our 401(k) examples, you would end up with $246,036.41. When we take out your total contributions of $66,000, you're left with earnings of $180,036.41. You need to pay capital gains tax on this money, and we'll assume you're in the 15% bracket and not the 20%.

In this simple example, you would save $27,005.46 in taxes. Wow! Thank you, Uncle Sam, for creating the 529 college savings plan. This $27,005.46 saved on taxes stretches our earnings and helps us achieve our goals faster. The second type of 529 plan is a prepaid tuition plan.

Prepaid Tuition Plan

Prepaid tuition plans run through the states, and you can partici-pate in any of the states' programs. However, you may get a state income tax break if you participate in your own state's plan. With a prepaid tuition plan, you lock in tuition at current rates for your child, who may not be attending for many years in the future. The advantage of a prepaid tuition plan is locking in the current tuition rates and, as we learned earlier, from 2000 to 2020, average college tuition inflation outpaced wage inflation by 111.4%. Locking cur-rent tuition rates is significant and worth exploring.

Both of these 529 college savings plans have advantages. Choosing one of them is a great option for paying for your child's or children's college education. I know firsthand when I say you won't regret starting as soon as your child is born and taking ad-vantage of the magic of compound interest along with the tax ad-vantages of a 529 college savings plan. Doing so will save you money, stretch your earnings, and help you achieve your goals faster.

How Do I Take Action?

First, you need to decide if you want to participate in an education savings plan or'a prepaid tuition plan. Education savings plans are a more common choice. It probably has to do with the ability to be more flexible with how much and when you make contributions. Let's look at how you would implement both, starting with a prepaid tuition plan.

Prepaid Tuition Plan

I chose the prepaid tuition plan. Please remember that just because I chose this option doesn't mean you should. To be truthful, it's been more than 16 years since I invested my money in this plan, and when I analyze the current numbers, I would have been better off investing the money in a traditional educational savings plan. Every family situation is different. Sixteen years ago, when I analyzed both options, based on my situation at the time, I felt the prepaid tuition plan was right for my family. We chose this program because we knew we would have only one child, and I had the money upfront to pay for it.

I live in Illinois, so I chose the College Illinois! 529 prepaid tuition plan. I filled out the paperwork and had to decide on a payment plan. There were several options. These included monthly installment payments over numerous years, lump sum payments over a few years, and one lump sum payment. The longer you chose to make payments, the more expensive it was to lock in the current tuition rates.

Because I was interested in stretching my earnings and because I had the money, I made two lump sum payments over two years. At the time, it was $20,000 right after my son was born and $20,000 when he was a year old. I chose this payment plan because $20,000 was the most you could write off on your income taxes, and it was less expensive than a longer-period payment plan. This also saved me money over two years on my state income taxes.

If my son goes to a public school in Illinois, his tuition is paid for through this program. This is true regardless of how much tuition outpaces inflation.

If my son goes to a school outside of Illinois, the program takes the weighted average tuition of in-state public universities and sends a check for that amount to the college my son chooses to attend. If the out-of-state tuition is more than the weighted average of Illinois schools, the balance will be on me. In full disclosure, this pays for tuition, but I still need to pay for room and board and books.

This is still a wonderful program because I was able to lock in current tuition rates the year my son was born. When my son goes to school 19 years later, tuition will be significantly higher.

Most prepaid tuition plans in other states work very similarly to the Illinois plan. Take a look to see if your state offers a plan.

Education Savings Plans
As described earlier, the second and most common option you need to learn about is a traditional 529 education savings plan. First, you need to know how much money you'll need for your child's college education without taking out any loans. There are numerous college cost calculators to be found through a simple search online. Look at Figure 8-6 as an example of a college calculator to see the information or values you'll need to determine.

Once you determine the values, the calculator will show you how much college will cost for your child in the future. It will also show you how much you'll need to save every month so you won't have to borrow the money when the time comes.

This is the starting point. You need to have a good estimate of how much it'll cost before moving forward. This helps with that first step.

Figure 8-6[23]

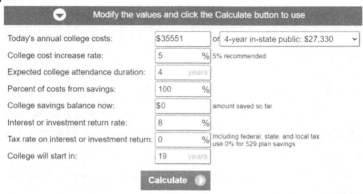

You can go back to this calculator periodically as your unborn child turns into a baby, toddler, or teenager to update the values and see how you're financially doing on your goal. This will give you more information and help you decide if you need to contribute more money to your 529 plan.

Similar to starting early to invest for retirement, put compound interest and time on your side by starting to invest for college when your child is born. The sooner you start, the less you'll need per month to pay for college. We learned this lesson in Action 1 where we invest early for retirement.

Now you'll need to set up a 529 college savings account. You have several options. One is to have a financial adviser help you. Another is to go directly to an investment company like Fidelity, T. Rowe Price, or Vanguard (there are many other options) and choose your investment (mutual funds) within the investment company.

You'll also need to fill out the paperwork for a 529 college savings account so you can take advantage of the wonderful tax benefits. This paperwork is quite simple, and you can always call the investment company of your choice if you need help. I've found the help from them over the phone to be very helpful.

Now you need to fund the investment. Most of these accounts will have an automated option where monthly contributions come out of your account automatically to make things less stressful.

Please don't put this off for years or even months because you're not sure which company is the "best" option for you. This only delays the amount of time you have to come up with a large sum of money. Do some research and decide where you want to have your 529 savings plan so you can get started. You won't regret doing this when the time comes to pay for your child's education.

You should know that you control the account once you set it up on behalf of your future college student. You retain control at all times and can change the beneficiary at any time, increase or decrease contributions, and access the money tax-free when used for educational purposes. You can also roll unused money from 529 plans over to a Roth IRA tax-free.

I often get asked, "Should I max out my 401(k) first, or contribute to the 529 savings plan?" While this depends on your answers to your goals in Action 7, I would max out my 401(k) contribution first and then work on the 529 college savings plan.

Congratulations on funding your 529 plan! You won't regret it when your cute little baby heads off to college down the road.

Action 40

I will set forth my wishes in
a last will and testament.

Background Knowledge

Last Will and Testament – Legal document that sets forth your wishes for the care of your children along with the distribution of your property and other assets.

Executor – The person you choose to handle the wishes set out in your will.

Heirs – The person or persons legally entitled to inherit the property or money from your estate.

Medical Power of Attorney – The person you trust to make medical decisions for you when you're mentally unable to.

Why Should I Take Action?

Some people think a will is only necessary for the rich or people with complex estates. This is simply not true. What would happen if you and your spouse passed away in a tragic accident? Who would raise your children? Who would get your home, cars, money, and other assets? Who do you want to leave a specific heirloom to?

Failure to prepare a will can leave decisions about your children and assets in the hands of judges and the courts. Do you really want to put your loved ones through this nightmare? The best way to make sure your wishes are carried out is to have a last will and testament.

There are also some other advantages to a will, such as saving money on taxes and fewer headaches for your heirs. For example, they will get access to your estate much more quickly if it's not tied up in the courts. I strongly believe you should have a will drawn up when you have children. You can decide if you want to have one earlier or not. Don't delay. TAKE ACTION!! You just never know when something tragic can happen to you and/or your spouse.

How Do I Take Action?

While you can prepare a will yourself and have it witnessed and signed by others to make it more official and less likely to be challenged, I recommend that you consider spending the money to have your will done by a trust and estate attorney. These people specialize in this work and do it every single day. When my wife and I had our will done, our attorney asked questions that we never even considered. Our will is much more complete and thorough because of it. It also is a legal document that will hold up in court because our lawyer knew the legal language to use in such a document. They know the law.

Prices will vary from lawyer to lawyer and from state to state based on how simple or complex your estate is. Prices generally range from $300 to $1,000 for people who don't have complex estates. If you can't afford this, at least write a will yourself and have it signed by two other people.

Some things to consider in your will include:

- Who do you want to raise your children if both you and your spouse pass away?
- Who do you want to be your executor?
- Who do you want to be your medical power of attorney?
- Do you want to prorate your assets to your children at specific

ages with specific percentages of your assets? In other words, this makes sure your children don't get what could be a significant amount of money at an early age like 18 or 21.

- What do you want to happen with your estate if everyone in your family (you, spouse, children) all pass away in a horrific accident?

- Do you have specific family heirlooms like a wedding ring, other jewelry, or antiques that you want to go to a specific person?

- How do you want to divide up your money? Equal percentages or not?

These are all tough decisions that should be thoughtfully discussed with your spouse. My wife and I felt a sense of calm and peace of mind knowing our wishes were all discussed and put in writing. I believe you'll also feel this peace of mind after you've thoroughly discussed and have a last will and testament finished.

Afterword

Thank you for taking this journey with me. My hope for you after reading this book is that you feel energized and understand that you have control of your own future. This is true regardless of how much money you make. Remember, it's not how much you make but what you do with the money you make.

The financial decisions you make moving forward will have a major impact on your life. Implementing these action statements will help you be successful by consciously setting your life goals and letting those goals be the driving force behind your day-to-day financial decisions. Doing this will give you a sense of fulfillment and control as opposed to the frustrating feeling that comes from emotional impulse buying.

Your journey is not over. I encourage you to keep seeking, learning, and continue being informed. The most important investment you will ever make is an investment in yourself. Become a lifelong learner. Go back and reread sections of this book to help you stay the course. Doing this will remind you of all the daily important decisions that need your attention. Also, go back and reread sections when you're performing the action in question. For example, go back and reread the Buying a Car section every time you purchase a car

Now that you've read this book, I think you have a pretty good feel for who I am and what's important to me. I also think you know what I would and would not do when making financial decisions.

As a result, I'm going to close the same way I closed every single class session I taught. When the bell rang, I would yell out in a very loud, energetic voice, "Have a wonderful day, and for goodness' sake, don't do anything I wouldn't do out there!"

Good luck to you, and go out and chart your course in life.

Acknowledgments

I truly feel blessed to have been given so many gifts in my life. One of these is the gift of inquisitiveness. To this day, I ask a lot of questions in order to explore, grow and learn. I am blessed with a very large extended family with five brothers and sisters and a small army of nieces and nephews. Most of my nieces and nephews are in their 20s and 30s, and I thought of them as I wrote this book. I'm also blessed that my wife and I have always been on the same page as far as our financial goals. We walk in unison, which makes life so much more wonderful and less stressful. I'm thankful for my wife and our life together.

This book would not have been possible without the help of countless people. I've made a conscious decision to spend time with people who help me grow and make me better. People who lift me up. I feel blessed to have a great team of people who helped me turn this book into a reality. Their fingerprints are all over this book.

I'm grateful to Mike Sansone, my editor, who is incredibly skilled and helped me by asking thought-provoking questions and making suggestions that made the book flow better.

The following individuals were willing to share their stories, experiences, and expertise for the book: Matt Blum, Steve Braun, Natalie Freund, Tom Gladfelter, Dawn Hall, and Drew Hettermann.

Experts in their fields have given generously of their time and talent in helping me make sure this book depicts an accurate account of how things work in the real world. A huge thank you to Erin Conway, Ryan Conway, Gregg Fields, Scott Freund, Sue

Miller, John Jenkins, and Joe Vidmar. You are truly amazing professionals who gave wonderful examples for me to use throughout the book.

Scott Freund, John Jenkins, and Joe Vidmar also read the section of the book that related to their expertise and offered valuable insights. Natalie Freund, Drew Hettermann, and Mike Sansone read the whole book and offered their suggestions. I cannot thank these six people enough, as their suggestions ultimately made the book more thorough and, quite frankly, better.

Technology is not a strength of mine, so I sought out support from Lisa Meinhard Sly, who is both knowledgeable and a wonderful teacher of technology. I also owe Lisa a debt of gratitude for going the extra mile and ultimately coming up with the final version of the book cover. She along with a small army of my family and friends helped flesh out the cover from beginning to end and ultimately made it better than I could have done by myself.

Thank you to Vince Font from Glass Spider Publishing. I thoroughly enjoyed working with you and appreciate your expertise, demeanor, and customer service personality.

Finally, I owe a debt of gratitude to all of the wonderful students I had the privilege of teaching. You, along with my son, are the inspiration that set the wheels in motion for the thought process that led to this book. I truly would not have written this without you.

Thank you all!

About the Author

Gary Freund spent thirty-three years as a business teacher and administrator in six different high-performing high schools. He feels blessed to have found his calling in life. His true passion has always been helping young adults understand the importance of the financial choices they make in life.

When he wasn't busy working with high schoolers, Gary bought, rehabbed, and rented out single-family homes and duplexes with his brother. They also owned a wholesale dry cleaning plant. These invaluable experiences played a key role in shaping who he is today. He has a bachelor's degree and two master's degrees and lives with his wife and son in the suburbs of Chicago. They love to travel and spend time with their extended family.

www.garyfreund.com

Gary welcomes the opportunity to hear how the financial concepts in this book have helped its readers, and how he can make future editions more helpful. He also would love to hear from teachers who are using the book in their classroom. Visit his website to get in touch.

Gary's engaging talks on personal finance at conferences, libraries, and universities inspire attendees to take control of their financial future. Contact him through his website to discover more about his impactful presentations.

If you enjoyed this book, please leave a review on Amazon, Barnes and Noble, Goodreads, or your favorite online book retailer website.

Index

Endnotes

[1] "Range of Stock, Bond, and Blended Total Returns." J.P. Morgan Private Bank. Last modified March 21, 2023. www.privatebank.jpmorgan.com/gl/en/insights/investing/4-charts-to-help-put-todays-turmoil-in-perspective

[2] Booth, David. "Two steps forward, one step back for investors." Firstlinks. Last modified February 22, 2023. www.firstlinks.com.au/two-steps-forward-one-step-back-investors

[3] "Social Security Fact Sheet." Social Security Administration. www.ssa.gov/news/press/factsheets/basicfact-alt.pdf

[4] Sommer, Jeff. "Mutual Funds That Consistently Beat the Market? Not One of 2,132." The New York Times. Last modified December 2, 2022. www.nytimes.com/2022/12/02/business/stock-market-index-funds.html

[5] Miller, Stephen. "401(k) Plan Match Formulas and Automatic Features Add Value for Participants." SHRM. Last modified July 9, 2021. www.shrm.org/resourcesandtools/hr-topics/benefits/pages/401k-plan-match-formulas-automatic-features-add-value-for-participants.aspx

[6] Frankel, Matthew. "1 in 5 Americans Are Making a Terrible 401(k) Mistake." The Motley Fool. Last modified February 9, 2018. www.fool.com/investing/2018/02/09/1-in-5-americans-are-making-a-terrible-401k-mistak.aspx

[7] Davis, Greg. "Our chief investment officer's take on the markets." Vanguard. Last modified September 26, 2022. www.investor.vanguard.com/investor-resources-education/news/our-chief-investment-officers-take-on-the-markets.

[8] "Timing the Market Is Impossible." Hartford Funds, Feb. 2023. www.hartfordfunds.com/practice-management/client-conversations/managing-volatility/timing-the-market-is-impossible.html

[9] www.lazyportfolioetf.com/etf/spdr-sp-500-spy-rolling-returns

[10] Ward, Judith. "Why Purposeful Asset Allocation Is Key for Long-Term Success." T. Rowe Price. Last modified August 5, 2022. www.troweprice.com/personal-investing/resources/insights/asset-allocation-planning-for-retirement.html

[11] Proctor, Clint. "What Is a Bad Credit Score and What Is Considered Bad Credit?" Business Insider. Last modified February 2, 2023. www.businessinsider.com/personal-finance/what-is-a-bad-credit-score

[12] Farley, Jess. "Tips for Managing Your Credit Score." Award Wallet. Last modified January 13, 2017. www.awardwallet.com/blog/tips-managing-credit-score

[13] Board of Governors of the Federal Reserve System (US), Federal Funds Effective Rate [FEDFUNDS], retrieved from FRED, Federal Reserve Bank of St. Louis; www.fred.stlouisfed.org/series/FEDFUNDS, April 10, 2024.

[14] "Mortgage Rates Tick Down." Freddie Mac. Last modified May 4, 2023. www.freddiemac.com/pmms/pmms30

[15] Dunn, Andrew. "What is the average home value increase per year?" Credit Karma, 30 Aug. 2022. www.creditkarma.com/home-loans/i/average-home-value-increase-per-year

[16] www.hemortgagereports.com/61853/30-year-mortgage-rates-chart

[17] Peterson, Bailey. "Current Average Real Estate Commission." Clever. Last modified April 21, 2023. www.listwithclever.com/average-real-estate-commission-rate

[18] www.wallethub.com/edu/ci/how-much-does-insurance-go-up-after-an-accident/87986

[19] Norman, Kayda. "Does a Speeding Ticket Affect Your Insurance?" NerdWallet. Last modified April 27, 2023. www.nerdwallet.com/article/insurance/auto-insurance-rates-after-speeding-ticket

[20] Russo, Kristina. "How Much Should You Spend on an Engagement Ring in 2022?" American Express. Last modified February 14, 2022. www.americanexpress.com/en-us/credit-cards/credit-intel/engagement-ring-cost

[21] "Umbrella Insurance." Childress Insurance Agency. www.childressinsuranceagency.com/umbrella.php

[22] Hanson, Melanie. "Average Cost of College & Tuition." Education Data Initiative. Last modified April 3, 2023. www.educationdata.org/average-cost-of-college

[23] www.calculator.net/college-cost-calculator.html

Printed in the USA
CPSIA information can be obtained
at www.ICGtesting.com
LVHW011206150824
788288LV00001B/2